THE
WRITER'S
VOICE

BY THE SAME AUTHOR

GENERAL

Under Pressure: The Writer in Society: Eastern Europe and the USA
The Savage God: A Study of Suicide
Life After Marriage: Scenes from Divorce
The Biggest Game in Town
Offshore: A North Sea Journey
Feeding the Rat: Profile of a Climber
Rain Forest (with paintings by Charles Blackman)
Night: An Exploration of Night Life, Night Language,
Sleep and Dreams
Poker: Bets, Bluffs and Bad Beats

AUTOBIOGRAPHY
Where Did It All Go Right?

NOVELS
Hers
Hunt
Day of Atonement

POETRY
Lost
Penguin Modern Poets, No. 18
Apparition (with paintings by Charles Blackman)
Autumn to Autumn and Selected Poems 1953–1976
New and Selected Poems

CRITICISM
The Shaping Spirit (US title: Stewards of Excellence)
The School of Donne
Beyond All This Fiddle: Essays 1955–1967
Samuel Beckett

ANTHOLOGIES (EDITOR)
The New Poetry
The Faber Book of Modern European Poetry

THE WRITER'S VOICE

AL ALVAREZ

BLOOMSBURY

LONDON · BERLIN · NEW YORK

First printed in Great Britain 2005
This paperback edition published 2006

Copyright © 2005 by A. Alvarez

Bloomsbury Publishing Plc, 36 Soho Square, London W1D 3QY

Bloomsbury Publishing, London, Berlin and New York

A CIP catalogue record is available from the British Library

ISBN 978 0 7475 7931 1

10 9 8 7 6 5 4 3

FSC
Mixed Sources
Product group from well-managed
forests and other controlled sources
Cert no. SGS-COC-2061
www.fsc.org
© 1996 Forest Stewardship Council

The paper this book is printed on is certified independently in accordance with the
rules of the FSC. It is ancient-forest friendly. The printer holds chain of custody.

Printed by Clays Ltd, St Ives plc

www.bloomsbury.com/alalvarez

To Jane and Vincent

CONTENTS

Preface
9

Chapter 1
FINDING A VOICE
13

Chapter 2
LISTENING
46

Chapter 3
THE CULT OF PERSONALITY AND THE
MYTH OF THE ARTIST
76

Acknowledgments   122
Notes   123

PREFACE

My subject is imaginative writing and how to read it: first, how a writer develops a voice of his own and a presence on the page; then, how the reader learns to hear that voice and respond; and finally, how the true voice and the public personality sometimes clash, confuse, and contradict each other.

For a writer, voice is a problem that never lets you go, and I have thought about it for as long as I can remember —if for no other reason than that a writer doesn't properly begin until he has a voice of his own. Young writers hoping to cut a figure on the scene often confuse voice with stylishness, but that is something quite different from a voice with the whole weight of a life, however young, behind it, the one Jane Kramer calls "the voice that you can't quite hear . . . that, with any luck, will eventually start to sound like you." A voice of that kind changes as you change, and what you do with it once you have it depends on character as well as talent and inclination. Some people write because they are Ancient Mariners with stories they are compelled to tell or lessons they have to teach; others, less lovable, because they are entranced by the sound of their own voices. For freelance writers like myself who belong to an endangered species which, as long ago as 1949, Cyril Connolly was already calling "the last known herd in existence of that mysterious animal, 'the English man of letters,'" writing is less a compulsion than a misfortune, like a doomed love affair. We write because we fell in love with language when we were young and impressionable, just as musicians fall in love with sound, and thereafter are doomed to explore this fatal attraction in as many ways as we can.

So what I have to say is based on a lifetime of trying to write in several different genres: poems, novels, and, above all, the kind of higher journalism that universities sometimes dignify as "the literature of fact": nonfiction books on subjects that happened to interest me—anything from suicide to poker, by way of divorce, dreams, offshore oil, and mountaineering—several of which began as long pieces for *The New Yorker*. I have also written a great deal of literary criticism which, when I was starting out half a century ago, had not yet become just another arcane academic discipline with a technical vocabulary and specialized interests all its own. It was thought of, instead, as a creative activity in its own right—a writer's way of describing how other writers handle language and what it is that makes them unique.

I sometimes feel about my profession much the same as Vladimir Mayakovsky felt about suicide: "I do not recommend it to others," he wrote, and then put a gun to his head. Freelance writing is a precarious trade, not least because shifting from one literary form to another may mean you end up mastering none. But for a writer, even precariousness has its uses: if nothing else, it makes you constantly alert to the way your voice comes off the page. The art of poetry is altogether different from that of prose, just as writing fiction is different from writing nonfiction, and literary criticism is different from them all. Fifty years of writing for a living have taught me that there is only one thing the four disciplines have in common: in order to write well you must first learn how to listen. And that, in turn, is something writers have in common with their readers. Reading well means opening your ears to the presence behind the words and knowing which notes are true and which are false. It is as much an art as writing well and almost as hard to acquire.

Chapter 1

FINDING A VOICE

The Genius of Poetry must work out its own salvation in a
man: it cannot be matured by law and precept, but by
sensation and watchfulness in itself.

—KEATS

i

W hat happens when you sit down with a book?
Why do you do it? What's the pleasure in it?
Why do books, poems, even fragments go on
being read years, sometimes centuries, after they were written, and look like they will continue to be read no matter
how many times the death of literature is announced?

I'm not talking about transmitting or acquiring information. On the contrary, at this present moment of change,
when the industrial revolution has been superseded by a
revolution in information technology, facts and figures have
never been easier to come by, although now they are pack-
aged in an appropriately new form. Computers, for example, no longer come with handbooks; all that kind of
information is built in; if you want to know how to do
something, you click "Help" and, if necessary, print up what
you find for future reference. Eventually, I assume, that is

how most reference books will be, and the advantages, in terms of economy and convenience, are greater than the drawbacks. Staring at a computer screen in your living room may be no substitute for the silence and calm of a library, and surfing the Web with Google is not as satisfying as rummaging in the stacks, but for those who can't afford to buy, say, the *Encyclopaedia Britannica*, and lack the yard or two of shelf space to accommodate it, it is better to have the work on CD-ROM or the Web, complete with sounds and moving pictures and hyperlinks, than not to have it at all.

Computers may be convenient and efficient, but they are not quite the neutral instruments they seem to be, and the subtle deformations they create in our attitude to language can be dangerous to literature:

> A philologist and his wife for dinner ... His ambition is to determine, by the use of electrical computation machines, the basic structure of language. Word values and evocations can be determined, he tells me, by machinery, and thus successful poetry can be written by machines. So we get back to the obsolescence of the sentiments. I think of my own sense of language, its intimacy, its mysteriousness, its power to evoke, in a catarrhal pronunciation, the sea winds that blow across Venice or in a hard "A" the massif beyond Kitzbühel. But this, he tells me, is all sentimentality. The importance of these machines, the drive to legislate, to calibrate words like "hope," "courage," all the terms we use for the spirit.[1]

John Cheever wrote that some time in the 1950s, long before computers were just another domestic accessory, even before they had a proper name. The philologist's reductive arrogance and the author's outraged response are opposing reactions to a simple truth that still applies: information and imaginative writing are different forms of knowledge, demanding different skills and wholly different attitudes to language.

In order to acquire facts efficiently, scan a synopsis, or gut a newspaper, you have to master the art of reading diagonally. Real literature is about something else entirely and it's immune to speed-reading. That is, it's not about information, although you may gather information along the way. It's not even about storytelling, although sometimes that is one of its greatest pleasures. Imaginative literature is about listening to a voice. When you read a novel the voice is telling you a story; when you read a poem it's usually talking about what its owner is feeling; but neither the medium nor the message is the point. The point is that the voice is unlike any other voice you have ever heard and it is speaking directly to you, communing with you in private, right in your ear, and in its own distinctive way. It may be talking to you from centuries ago or from a few years back or, as it were, from across the room—bang up-to-date in the here and now. The historical details are secondary; all that really matters is that you hear it—an undeniable presence in your head, and still very much alive, no matter how long ago the words were spoken:

Western wind, when wilt thou blow
That the small rain down can rain?
Christ, if my love were in my arms
And I in my bed again!

Nobody knows who wrote that poem or even precisely when he wrote it (probably early in the sixteenth century). But whoever it was is still very much alive—lonely, miserable, hunkered down against the foul weather and a long way from home, yearning for spring and warmth and his girl. Across a gap of five centuries, the man is still our contemporary.

Writing, I mean, is literally a lively art as well as a creative one. Writers don't just "hold, as 'twere, a mirror up to nature" by creating an imitation of life; they create a moment of life itself. That anonymous poet has left the sound of his voice on the air as distinctly as, say, van Eyck fixed forever the tender marriage of Arnolfini and his wife in paint. The poem breathes from the page as vividly as the long-dead faces and their little dog breathe from the canvas. But it is a two-way pact: the writer makes himself heard and the reader listens in—or, more accurately, the writer works to find or create a voice that will stretch out to the reader, make him prick his ears and attend.*

ii

I think this process is something like what happens in psychoanalysis. Of course, there has always been a close connection between imaginative literature and the talking cure, not least because Freud himself read widely and

* Etymologically, "attend" is a submerged metaphor. It comes from the Latin words *ad*, meaning "to" or "toward," and *tendere*, "to stretch." When I attend to you, I stretch my ears toward you.

wrote compelling prose. Both these accomplishments were unusual in a scientist and they generated in him an even more unusual respect for the arts. When, during the celebration of his seventieth birthday, one of his disciples hailed Freud as "the discoverer of the unconscious," he answered, "The poets and philosophers before me discovered the unconscious. What I discovered was the scientific method by which the unconscious can be studied."[2]

In the early years, psychoanalysts often seemed to take this connection in a literal, straightforward way. Freud, with his interest in archaeology, labored to dig up the past and re-create it, almost as a work of art. It was as if psychoanalysis were a kind of dual storytelling: the patient told his story from his point of view and the analyst told it back to him, using his interpretations to give it a new shape and meaning. Freud may have called his method scientific, but, in practice, he worked more like a novelist than a researcher, creating form and significance out of the chaos of the unconscious, especially as it expresses itself in dreams, the one area in which the imagination of even the most unimaginative people reveals itself.

And because dreams, in their dotty way, seem creative, this led to a fundamental misunderstanding of the nature of art, particularly in the early days of psychoanalysis when the idea of sexual symbolism was still fresh and exciting and subversive. Instead of reading, say, a poem as a work of art with a life of its own, independent of the author—as something which, in Coleridge's words, "contains in itself the reasons why it is so and not otherwise"[3]—psychoanalysts with a taste for literature often used it as though it were mere dream stuff, welling up uncensored and unbidden, another royal road to the unconscious of the unfortunate author.

A century later, psychoanalysts tend to be less interested in telling stories or creating an archaeology of the unconscious by digging up the past. They have broadened their focus to study not just the patient's self and his history but his whole inner world. Because this inner world includes both his self and what analysts call his "internal objects"— imaginative representations of other people, both past and present, with whom the patient is continually entangled— the therapist's task is to study how these "phantasy" figures are projected in the transference and countertransference—that is, in the minute changes in the relationship between the patient and the analyst as they occur, moment by moment, in the consulting room.

From this more modern perspective, the story matters less than how it is told. Instead of looking for clues, the therapist is listening, like a poet or a critic, to the overtones and undertones, alert to the false notes, to whatever is off-key or flat, distinguishing between the genuine emotions and the fake, monitoring when and how and why he is moved and—equally important—when and why he is bored. It's about detail and nuance—the body language and the silences, what is said and what is left unsaid. And as with literature, everything depends on the tone of voice. The object of the exercise for both the patient and the analyst is to listen for the true-speaking self among all the inauthentic ones, to find it and then to stick with it—without bluster or pretence or repetitiveness or excuses. In terms of concentration and openness to experience, and because both of them are ultimately concerned with truth to feeling, the psychoanalyst in search of a talking cure and the writer in search of a voice seem to be dealing, as delicately as they can, with similar problems. And occasionally—very occasionally—a psychoanalytic interpretation can be as intuitive and creative as a work of art.

As an art form, however, psychoanalysis has little to do with imaginative writing and a great deal in common with literary criticism. Or rather, with criticism as it used to be in the days before it was highjacked by extraliterary preoccupations such as theory, politics, gender, race, and, indeed, psychoanalysis. True criticism, the kind practiced by masters like Coleridge and T. S. Eliot, comes without much theoretical baggage and with little to prove. In order to find out what's going on in a work of art, the critic must let go of his own sensibility and immerse himself in that of another writer, without theories and without preconceptions. All that is required of him is attention and detachment—an attentive state of detachment—listening, thinking, and giving himself up all at the same time. And that, I assume, is much the same as the "evenly suspended attention" with which, said Freud, the therapist listens to a patient.[4]

It is here that the analyst and the critic join the creative artist. Like psychoanalysis, the arts are complex disciplines, crafts that take years to acquire. But once this long apprenticeship is over and the technical skills are so perfected that they have become instinctive, a strange transformation takes place: as the artist becomes absorbed in the practical details of his craft, his personality recedes and the work cuts itself free of its maker, acquiring a separate life of its own. Coleridge put it best when he described Shakespeare in full flow: "himself meanwhile unparticipating in the passions, and actuated only by that pleasurable excitement, which had resulted from the energetic fervour of his own spirit in vividly exhibiting what it had so accurately and profoundly contemplated."[5] Coleridge's word for this style of creative detachment was "aloofness," and it is a quality that doesn't come easily or often. But when it does, the effect on both writer and reader is strangely liberating.

This is why D. H. Lawrence was wrong, I think, when he wrote, "One sheds one's sicknesses in books—repeats and presents one's emotions to be master of them." Art is about more than compensation and self-therapy, just as psychoanalysis is about more than relieving symptoms, and cure is too narrow a concept for what either can do at its best. Repeat, best. A good poem is as hard to find as a good analysis, but, once found, the effect of both is to make you—the reader, the patient—more fully and pleasurably alive.

The writer discovers this liberating and oddly invigorating relationship between psychic reality and aesthetic pleasure when he finds his own voice: it picks the locks, opens the doors, and enables him to begin to say what he wants to say. But in order to find his voice he must first have mastered style, and style, in this basic sense, is a discipline that you acquire by hard work, like grammar and punctuation. (It can also be a trap that lures you into symptoms of a different kind—mannerism or the formal cadences of high rhetoric. I will return to this later.) Voice is altogether different: "I don't mean style . . . ," Philip Roth wrote, in *The Ghost Writer*, "I mean voice: something that begins at around the back of the knees and reaches well above the head." Voice, he means, is the vehicle by which a writer expresses his aliveness, and Roth himself is all voice. Style, in the formal or flowery sense, bores him; he has, he has written, a "resistance to plaintive metaphor and poeticised analogy."[6] His prose is immaculate yet curiously plain and unostentatious, at once unselfconscious and unmistakably his own. Someone once said that reading him is like opening a cellar door and hearing the boiler roar into life. It's also like being pitched headfirst into a family quarrel, with everyone shouting to be heard; it makes your heart contract with outrage and excitement both at once.

Freud, too, had a voice, and reading him is a pleasure, even for the layman, which is one of the many reasons why he remains a powerful figure. You may read the works of later influential psychoanalysts, like Melanie Klein and Wilfred Bion, for their ideas, but you read them with gritted teeth because they handle language so clumsily. Or rather, they handle it with distaste, like scientists on the far side of the divide between the two cultures, for whom language is a necessary but inadequate medium, not worthy of their attention, the straw from which they are grudgingly forced to make their bricks. Yet it was Freud, not Klein or Bion, who thought of himself as a scientist and set out to discover "the scientific method by which the unconscious can be studied." But because he had learned from "the poets and philosophers before me" and respected what they had to say, he also respected the way in which they said it and followed their example. Hence the clarity of his language and his vivid presence on the page, quizzically leading the reader on from one point in the argument to the next, following it wherever it went, regardless of his own preconceptions, and driving each point home with case histories as intricate and involving as fiction.

Freud himself was baffled by his literary gifts and by the relative absence of scientific paraphernalia and jargon in his work:

> I have not always been a psychotherapist. Like other neuro-pathologists, I was trained to employ local diagnoses and electro-prognosis, and it still strikes me myself as strange that the case histories I write should read like short stories and that, as one might say, they lack the serious stamp of science. I must console myself with the reflection that the nature of the subject is evidently responsible for this, rather than any preference of my own. The fact is that local diagnosis and electrical reactions lead nowhere in the study of hysteria, whereas a detailed description of mental processes such as we are accustomed to find in the works of imaginative writers enables me, with the use of a few psychological formulas, to obtain at least some kind of insight into the course of that affection.[7]

It is as though he were embarrassed to have found answers to what he was looking for in imaginative writing instead of the laboratory, and embarrassed, too, by his own literary talent—by the subtlety and relish with which he handles the clinical material, probing it for clues like a detective, sifting them, weighing them, linking them together in order to solve a mystery. The mystery, of course, is that of the unconscious—how things we don't know about ourselves soak through like rising damp, changing what we think we know and how we behave. But the mystery, and how Freud's solution altered our perception of the world, are not my business, even if I were qualified to discuss them. What matters to me as a writer is his tone of voice, the vigilance and persistence of his intellectual curiosity, and his refusal to disregard the life of the imagination, even in the cause of science. When you read Freud, you are listening to a brilliant man thinking on his feet, and that, as Coleridge said, is a "pleasurable excitement."

iii

By comparing writing and psychoanalysis, I'm implying that finding your own voice as a writer is in some ways like the tricky business of becoming an adult. For a writer, it's also a basic instinct, like a bird marking its territory, though not so straightforward or so musical. So how do you do it? First, you do what all young people do: you try on other people's personalities for size and you fall in love. Young writers, in fact, are a peculiarly promiscuous lot; my schoolboy passions included Eliot, Auden, Housman, Aldous Huxley, one after the other with scarcely a gap between them. Every so often serial promiscuity culminates in *le coup de foudre*: you hear a voice and recognize it and know it's for you just as surely as you recognize Miss Right across the room before you've ever spoken to her, even when—or especially when—she is hand in hand with Mr. Wrong. First, the writer's voice dazzles you and you read everything you can lay your hands on. If that doesn't cure you, the sickness goes critical and you become obsessed with the beloved's whole take on life: what he did, where he went, even the kind of people he slept with. You don't want to be *like* him, you want to *be* him. In retrospect, infatuation is as embarrassing as promiscuity, but for the writer it is a necessary part of the weary process of growing up. That's what happened to me with Aldous Huxley when I was at school and with William Empson and D. H. Lawrence when I got to Oxford. But literary infatuation is the same as other youthful infatuations: it doesn't last and it's hard to be friends afterward. These days, I still admire Empson in a guarded way, but, apart from a handful of stories and poems, I find Lawrence's shrill nagging almost intolerable. As W. H. Auden wrote in *The Sea and the Mirror*, "I am very glad I shall never / Be twenty and have to go through the business again, / The hours of fuss and fury, the conceit, the expense."

There are other writers whom you fall for and stay in love with. It happened to me when I was a schoolboy and was given a poem by John Donne to comment on. At that point I had never heard of Donne and I had to read the poem—"Witchcraft by a Picture"—several times before I began to understand it. But I was seduced, at first hearing, by the tone of voice. It was like listening to subtly charged talk, aroused, casual, witty, and restlessly argumentative, a curious mixture of logic and tenderness—real tenderness for real women with appetites and sweaty palms and unreliable temperaments. This, I felt, was how poetry should be—alive with feeling yet utterly unsentimental, and with nothing conventionally poetical about it. For a lusty adolescent, shut away in a monkish, sports-mad boarding school where love of poetry was not a weakness you confessed to, it was a revelation, love at first sight, and I never really got over it. I was sixteen when I first read Donne and we are still going strong more than half a century later.

Donne is like Shakespeare—a great writer, the kind T. S. Eliot said you can never hope to emulate, who is simply there to set the standards to which you inadequately aspire. The ones you imitate are usually less overpowering but they teach you the skills, the techniques, the tricks of the trade that you need to acquire during your literary apprenticeship, because until you have learned the basic skills you can't properly begin. But once you have found your own voice, you take the skills for granted and are free to use or discard them as you wish. You can also incorporate other people's voices into your own and still sound like yourself. That is what Eliot meant when he wrote, "Immature poets imitate; mature poets steal." The aphorism, of course, was a sly joke at his own expense because wholesale stealing was what Eliot had done in *The Waste Land*, where almost every other line was either a quote or a reference to another writer. Yet Eliot used the fragments for his own ends and in such an authoritative way that they now seem to belong more to him than to their authors. Since he believed strenuously in the classical impersonality of art, he would have claimed that his ragbag of quotations and references was merely a way of setting

off the fragmented culture of Europe after the First World
War against a spiritually richer and more rooted past. But
he made the fragments so much his own that they also
compose a splintered image of his private troubles, reflec-
tions in a shattered mirror, a Cubist self-portrait.

   To explain what I mean by learning from your betters,
let me give you a couple of personal examples. When I was
in my teens and keen to show how clever and sophisticated I was, I wrote what I thought was a really good
poem. It was about sex, of course, a subject I knew next to
nothing about, and it was full of sly allusions to mythology,
as smart poems were supposed to be in the late 1940s. The
poem is long gone—thrown away with other junk—but I
can still remember the penultimate quatrain:

> *The call of hounds moved Acteon*
> *To dream among suggestive trees.*
> *Light fed his ripe imagination*
> *Easy, divine virginities.*

The lines have stuck in my memory and not just because
this was the first poem I sent out into the world for publication, and therefore the first time my literary pride was
hurt when it was turned down. I remember the lines
because the editor of the little magazine I mailed it to sent
it back with an encouraging letter, calling that penultimate
quatrain "miraculous." Miraculous or not, I see now he
rejected the poem because he could hear behind it echoes
of Eliot's famous "Sweeney Among the Nightingales." If
so, he was right, though I was outraged at the time, of

course, and I still think the lines are pretty good for a teenager. Nevertheless, that one bit of praise from an authoritative stranger was all I needed to keep me going. And because he had picked out one stanza from several, I thought about why it worked and realized that it had something to do with the rhymes that weren't quite rhymes—Acteon/imagination, trees/virginities—rhymes that had come, as it were, of their own accord, without being worked for, like the half-rhymes and assonances blues singers constantly use: "I was born in a dump, / My momma died and my daddy got drunk." That, I realized, was something I had a knack for and could put to use. In those days, I hadn't read any poems by Wilfred Owen and knew nothing about his pararhymes. All I knew was that strict rhyme-schemes were too confining and too formal for the Modernist things I wanted to do, but I didn't trust free verse. Thereafter I often found myself using assonance as a kind of net to hold a poem together without drawing attention to itself. As it turned out, it took me a long time to find my own voice as a poet, but I think this was the first step.

In prose it took me even longer. The first time I realized I had found my own voice was in the introduction to a book called *Under Pressure*, which was published in 1965 and has long been out of print. It was based on a series of radio features I wrote for the BBC Third Programme on the writer in society in Eastern Europe and the USA. During the cold war, from 1961 to 1964, I traveled around some of the iron curtain countries—Poland, Hungary, Czechoslovakia, and Yugoslavia—recording conversations with poets, novelists, artists, and intellectuals about what it was like to work under acute political pressure. Then I went to the United States and did the same, though with a difference: I had already spent a lot of time in America and most of the people I spoke to were friends. Out of this mass of material I put together seven radio features, and features are in no way the same as talks. They are not one person saying his say but a medley of voices, all of them different—different accents, different intensities, different priorities—arranged on tape so that they seem to be arguing together, constantly interrupting and contradicting each other. And because I organized the material in such a way that they also seemed to be arguing with me, my own running commentary had to be similarly offhand. If I was going to join in—which I emphatically did—I couldn't lay down the law or pronounce *ex cathedra*, like a nervous lecturer reading from a text. I had to sound as casual and involved as everyone else. And that continual obligation to keep the tone easy stayed with me when I turned the broadcasts into a book.

Naturally, the introduction was written last, and when I read it over I thought, "That's how I should sound and how I want to sound." I remember being surprised. By then, I had already published a couple of books of literary criticism, but this was different—far more easygoing and immediate. It made me realize that I didn't much like the tone of voice I had used before; it seemed too cocksure, too pleased with itself, too self-consciously stylish. All that young man's elegance suddenly sounded defensive. It was a cop-out, I realized, because I hadn't really known who I was or what I was doing. Maybe I still didn't know, but at least I was beginning.

iv

The authentic voice may not be the one you want to hear. All true art is subversive at some level or other, but it doesn't simply subvert literary clichés and social conventions; it also subverts the clichés and conventions you yourself would like to believe in. Like dreams, it talks for parts of yourself you are not fully aware of and may not much like. Sometimes it goes against your daylight principles, though if you try to clean up your act you kill the life of what you have to say. That, presumably, is what Mayakovsky meant in a poem called "At the Top of My Voice," which he wrote not long before he committed suicide: "I / subdued / myself / setting my heel / on the throat / of my song"; he had throttled his inspiration for the good of the communist cause.

For Sylvia Plath the process was reversed. She served a long and stern apprenticeship with the masters who dominated the 1950s—first with Yeats and Wallace Stevens, then with Theodore Roethke, Robert Lowell, and her husband, Ted Hughes—and she published that apprentice work in her first collection, *The Colossus*. But the unique poems on which her reputation rests, all of them written in the last ten to twelve months of her life, were altogether freer, harsher, and more sardonic. "The Moon and the Yew Tree" is one of the first of them, and in it you can distinctly hear her authentic voice emerging:

This is the light of the mind, cold and planetary.
The trees of the mind are black. The light is blue.
The grasses unload their griefs on my feet as if I were God,
Prickling my ankles and murmuring of their humility.
Fumey, spiritous mists inhabit this place
Separated from my house by a row of headstones.
I simply cannot see where there is to get to.

The moon is no door. It is a face in its own right,
White as a knuckle and terribly upset.
It drags the sea after it like a dark crime; it is quiet
With the O-gape of complete despair. I live here.
Twice on Sunday, the bells startle the sky—
Eight great tongues affirming the Resurrection.
At the end, they soberly bong out their names.

The yew tree points up. It has a Gothic shape.
The eyes lift after it and find the moon.
The moon is my mother. She is not sweet like Mary.
Her blue garments unloose small bats and owls.
How I would like to believe in tenderness—
The face of the effigy, gentled by candles,
Bending, on me in particular, its mild eyes.

I have fallen a long way. Clouds are flowering
Blue and mystical over the face of the stars.
Inside the church, the saints will be all blue,
Floating on their delicate feet over the cold pews,
Their hands and faces stiff with holiness.
The moon sees nothing of this. She is bald and wild.

> *And the message of the yew tree is blackness—blackness and*
> *silence.*

This seems to me to be a poem in two voices—that of the disciplined, studious apprentice of high art and elegant prosody, and that of someone, or some thing, far less amenable. And these two voices speak out and clash continually throughout the poem. There are melodious, rhythmically elegant lines in the manner of Yeats:

> *How I would like to believe in tenderness—*
> *The face of the effigy, gentled by candles,*
> *Bending, on me in particular, its mild eyes.*

That sounds to me very similar in tone and movement to Yeats's "Among Schoolchildren":

> *Both nuns and mothers worship images,*
> *But those the candles light are not as those*
> *That animate a mother's reveries.*

Plath's mellifluousness, however, is constantly brought up short by bald, desolate statements in a bleakly speaking voice: "I simply cannot see where there is to get to," "I live here," "I have fallen a long way." It is almost as though the poem were written despite herself.

There are two notes about the genesis of this poem in Plath's *Collected Poems*. When Plath talked about it in a BBC radio broadcast, she said:

I did, once, put a yew tree in [a poem]. And that yew
tree began, with astounding egotism, to manage and
order the whole affair. It was not a yew tree by a church
on a road past a house in a town where a certain
woman lived . . . and so on, as it might have been in a
novel. Oh no. It stood squarely in the middle of my
poem, manipulating its dark shades, the voices in the
churchyard, the clouds, the birds, the tender melancholy
with which I contemplated it—everything! I couldn't
subdue it. And, in the end, my poem was a poem about
a yew tree. The yew tree was just too proud to be a
passing black mark in a novel.[8]

She's trying to make light of it, as though she were help-
lessly charmed by some baffling minor character who is
taking over the plot. Yet that's not at all how the poem
reads. The yew tree, in fact, doesn't appear until halfway
through the poem and there are only two lines specifically about it: first, "The yew tree points up. It has a
Gothic shape"; then, "And the message of the yew tree is
blackness—blackness and silence." This tree isn't proud or
fetching; it's downright menacing. And that fits the poem
fine because, as she declares at the start, what she is talking
about is a state of mind: "This is the light of the mind,
cold and planetary. / The trees of the mind are black." The
yew tree is a filter that changes what she calls "tender
melancholy"—the plangent mood that is reflected in
those sweet, Yeatsian cadences—into a blank and abrupt
despair. And maybe it does so because the yew tree, being
rooted in the cemetery at the end of her garden, reminds
her of death.

Ted Hughes's accompanying footnote in her *Collected Poems* is brief and factual:

> The yew tree stands in a churchyard to the west of the house in Devon, and visible from SP's bedroom window. On this occasion, the full moon, just before dawn, was setting behind this yew tree and her husband assigned her to write a verse "exercise" about it.

When Hughes and I were talking about this extraordinary poem, not long after Plath died, his version of the event was less laconic. He said that he had woken in the small hours to find Sylvia wandering around the bedroom, saying she couldn't sleep and complaining she had nothing to write about. He said irritably, "Why don't you look out the window and write about what you see?" Always the good student, she did what she was told. She dutifully set out to paint a nocturnal landscape and ended up with a picture of utter despair. When Hughes read the poem the following morning, he was appalled. Maybe Plath was too, but she had found her theme and the voice with which to express it, and she was on her way to the last great poems.

v

"The Moon and the Yew Tree" is a strong example of the difference between voice and style—between the formal art Plath had been trained in and the altogether livelier, starker voice she ended up with. High style, of course, has a long tradition: the subtitle of the most self-consciously stylish of all plays, John Lyly's *Euphues*, was *The Anatomy of Wit*, and flowery, learned wit was a skill much admired by fashionable young Elizabethans until Shakespeare ridiculed it in *Love's Labour's Lost*, a play written for an aristocratic audience who knew all about the art of rhetoric, and one in which ornate language matters more than the characters who speak it. Its heroes are courtly wits determined to show how witty they are, and their affectations are parodied by their lower class imitators—by the absurd flourishes of Armado, the "fantastical Spaniard," and the relentless pedantry of Holofernes, the schoolteacher, who have both "been at a great feast of languages and stolen the scraps." Shakespeare then tops them all with his own verbal and metrical pyrotechnics. In one form or another, linguistic ostentation is the fuel that drives the play forward and all parties are equally immodest. The difference is one of tone and manners—the courtier versus the pedant, elegance and edge versus braggadocio and vacuous circumlocution.

High style is the writer's equivalent of putting on airs and dropping names. According to the Irish novelist Aidan Higgins, Samuel Beckett, that most austere of writers, once compared "writing style, that vanity, . . . to a bow tie about a throat cancer." What is sometimes passed off as "fine writing"—also known as "poetic prose"—is usually little more than a set of secondhand stylistic devices that cost the writer nothing and flatter the readers into believing that, through it, they have graduated into a better class of literature. Fine writing indulged for its own sake also projects the image of an exquisite sensibility exposing itself for admiration in such a way that common sense gets shut out. For me, too much exposure to, say, Walter Pater aspiring to the condition of music or even to masters of high style like Wilde or Nabokov, who roll every syllable of every sentence around their tongues, sometimes makes me feel I'd kill for a casual remark or a touch of slang.

We all do it, of course, just as we all have other bad habits we fall into out of laziness. The secret is to catch yourself lapsing into your own rhetoric and turn away. "Never speak of 'my unconquerable soul' or of any vulgarism of that sort," wrote T. E. Hulme. "But thank God for the long note of the bugle, which moves all the world bodily out of the cinders and the mud." Hulme, whom Eliot called "the forerunner of a new attitude of mind, which should be called the twentieth-century mind," also wrote, "Always seek the hard, definite, personal word,"[9] and maybe that is what Karl Kraus was implying when he said, "My language is the universal whore whom I have to make into a virgin." Language is a whore because, left to itself, it turns the same old tired tricks with everyone. To restore its virginity you must first strip away the fancy clothes—the clichés, the tropes, the excesses—then you put the lady on a diet and reduce her to her bare essentials. According to Isaac Babel, "Your language becomes clear and strong, not when you can no longer add a sentence, but when you can no longer take away from it." Rudyard Kipling, who wrote some of the purest prose in the English language, said that when he finished a story he locked it away in a drawer for a few weeks, then went through it again, blacking out with Indian ink all the bits he had been most proud of the first time around.

To a psychiatrist, this unquenchable dissatisfaction and remorseless attention to detail—the continual writing and rewriting, paring away, purifying—might seem like a symptom of an obsessive-compulsive disorder. To the writer, it is simply part of the job, a necessary frustration to be endured when you try to adjust the slippery, imprecise medium of language to the precise pitch and cadence of your own voice. It is also a measure of aesthetic conscience, and that in itself is one of the pleasures of the creative process:

The great aim is accurate, precise and definite description. The first thing is to recognise how extraordinarily difficult this is. It is no mere matter of carefulness; you have to use language, and language is by its very nature a communal thing; that is, it expresses never the exact thing but a compromise—that which is common to you, me and everybody. But each man sees a little differently, and to get out clearly and exactly what he does see, he must have a terrific struggle with language, whether it be with words or the technique of other arts. Language has its own special nature, its own conventions and communal ideas. It is only by a concentrated effort of the mind that you can hold it fixed to your own purpose. I always think that the fundamental process at the back of all the arts might be represented by the following metaphor. You know what I call architect's curves—flat pieces of wood with all different kinds of curvature. By a suitable selection from these you can draw approximately any curve you like. The artist I take to be the man who simply can't bear the idea of that "approximately." He will get the exact curve of what he sees whether it be an object or an idea in the mind. I shall here have to change my metaphor a little to get the process in his mind. Suppose that instead of your curved pieces of wood you have a springy piece of steel of the same types of curvature as the wood. Now the state of tension or concentration of mind, if he is doing anything really good in this struggle against the ingrained habit of the technique, may be represented by a man employing all his fingers to bend the steel out of its own curve and into the exact curve which you want. Something different to what it would assume naturally.

There are then two things to distinguish, first the particular faculty of mind to see things as they really are, and apart from the conventional ways in which you have been trained to see them. This is itself rare enough in all consciousness. Second, the concentrated state of mind, the grip over oneself which is necessary in the actual expression of what one sees. To prevent one falling into the conventional curves of ingrained technique, to hold on through infinite detail and trouble to the exact curve you want. Wherever you get this sincerity, you get the fundamental quality of good art without dragging in infinite or serious. . . .

. . . Freshness convinces you, you feel at once that the artist is in an actual physical state. You feel that for a minute. Real communication is so very rare, for plain speech is unconvincing. It is in this rare fact of communication that you get the root of aesthetic pleasure.[10]

That is from T. E. Hulme's classic essay "Romanticism and Classicism," one of the most influential documents in the history of Modernism. Hulme himself was a poet only briefly and in passing,* yet apart from Coleridge's description in *Biographia Literaria* of Shakespeare at work, Hulme's, I think, is the subtlest and most inward account of the creative process ever written. And the secret is in the way what he is saying is reflected in the way he is saying it. Hulme writes like a man wholly at ease with himself, casually, conversationally, thinking on his feet, and trying to impress no one, intent only in expressing "the concentrated state of mind" and necessary "grip over oneself" through the cadences of his prose—just like the artist he describes. His cool, demystifying approach embodies the spirit of Modernism to which Eliot and Pound aspired, and his informality, so uncharacteristic of that stuffy period, makes him seem as contemporary now as he must have seemed when Eliot read him in the 1920s.

Here is a paradox: finding your own voice as a writer means—or is the equivalent of—feeling free in your own skin. It is a great liberation. Yet the only way to achieve it is through minute—the minutest—attention to detail: "A phrase is born into the world both good and bad at the same time. The secret lies in a slight, an almost invisible twist . . . ," wrote Babel. "No iron can stab the heart with such force as a period put just at the right place."[11] Here, for example, is Alice Monro at her deadly best: "His long

---

* His friend Ezra Pound published *The Complete Poetical Works of T. E. Hulme* as an appendix to his own collection, *Ripostes*, in 1912; it consisted of five short poems, and by the time it appeared, Hulme had more or less abandoned the art of poetry.

face was dignified and melancholy and he had something of the beauty of a powerful, discouraged, elderly horse."[12] "Discouraged" is not just vivid and apposite and unexpected, though it is all of those; it also brings to bear a whole freight load of insight and observation and experience that illuminates the author as well as the forgetful old man she is describing.

Auden, talking about verse forms, divided writers into two types:

> The difference between formal and free verse may be likened to the difference between carving and modelling; the formal poet, that is to say, thinks of the poem he is writing as something already latent in the language which he has to reveal, while the free verse poet thinks of language as a plastic passive medium upon which he imposes his artistic conception.[13]

In these terms, Flaubert, who labored for days on a single page, is the ultimate carver, and Balzac, who dashed off whole books in a few weeks, the ultimate modeler. Distinguishing between the carver and the modeler implies, of course, no value judgment; it has nothing to do with good writing or bad; it is simply a matter of different sensibilities. Samuel Beckett's Trappist austerity mirrors his chronic shyness as well as his bleak vision of the world, just as Henry James's convoluted style precisely reflects his notoriously hesitant manner of speaking—his way of constantly circling a topic, advancing upon it, then ceremoniously retreating, slowly moving a little closer, then closer still, sidling into range, preparing himself for the final definitive pounce. In real life, the Master's subtlety was harder to tolerate than in his fiction, and on one celebrated occasion it tried even the patience of his devoted friend and disciple, Edith Wharton:

James and I chanced to arrive at Windsor long after dark. We must have been driven by a strange chauffeur—perhaps Cook was on a holiday; at any rate, having fallen into the lazy habit of trusting to him to know the way, I found myself at a loss to direct his substitute to the King's Road. While I was hesitating, and peering out into the darkness, James spied an ancient doddering man who had stopped in the rain to gaze at us. "Wait a moment, my dear—I'll ask him where we are"; and leaning out he signalled to the spectator.

"My good man, if you'll be good enough to come here, please; a little nearer—so," and as the old man came up: "My friend, to put it to you in two words, this lady and I have just arrived here from *Slough*; that is to say, to be more strictly accurate, we have recently *passed through* Slough on our way here, having actually motored to Windsor from Rye, which was our point of departure; and the darkness having overtaken us, we should be much obliged if you would tell us where we now are in relation, say, to the High Street, which, as you of course know, leads to the Castle, after leaving on the left hand the turn down to the railway station."

I was not surprised to have this extraordinary appeal met by silence, and a dazed expression on the old wrinkled face at the window; nor to have James go on: "In short" (his invariable prelude to a fresh series of explanatory ramifications), "in short, my good man,

what I want to put to you in a word is this: supposing
we have already (as I have reason to think we have)
driven past the turn down to the railway station (which,
in that case, by the way, would probably not have been
on our left hand, but on our right), where are we now
in relation to . . ."

"Oh, please," I interrupted, feeling myself utterly
unable to sit through another parenthesis, "do ask him
where the King's Road is."

"Ah—? The King's Road? Just so! Quite right! Can
you, as a matter of fact, my good man, tell us where,
in relation to our present position, the King's Road
exactly *is*?"

"Ye're in it," said the aged face at the window.[14]

In life, James's pathological hesitancy was by turns absurd,
hilarious, and frustrating; in his novels, however, pathology
becomes a narrative device, a way of creating a delicate
web of insinuation by which he reveals his sly, sidelong
intimations of immorality. Adultery, for example, is never
exposed, it is merely hinted at. What Maisie knew about it
is an adult's mislaid umbrella and his sudden recollection
of where it has been left (at his mistress's apartment, but no
one says so). In *The Ambassadors*, all it takes for upright
Lambert Strether to understand that two charming friends
are sexually involved is a chance encounter with them out
boating on the Seine: they happen not to have coats to
protect them from the evening chill; ergo, they are not, like
him, enjoying an innocent day in the country; they have
left their other clothes at a riverside hotel; he, too, says not
a word, but his love affair with immoral Europe is over.

Tempests, for Henry James, are revealed only by the faintest cough of distant thunder over the horizon and out of sight.

Forthright or devious, there are as many rules for classy writing as there are for classy people, though the two categories do not necessarily overlap. "Some people have a native gift for using words, as some people have a naturally 'good eye' at games," wrote George Orwell. "It is largely a question of timing and of instinctively knowing how much emphasis to use."[15] It is also, in the end, a question of scrupulousness and conscience, an aesthetic morality that manifests itself in what Existentialists used to call "authenticity"—a sense of the weight of a whole person behind the words. True style—which is what I mean by voice—can come in any form provided it is alive and urgent enough to take hold of the reader and make him understand that what is being said really matters. Ford Madox Ford once said that, in his fiction, he aimed for "a limpidity of expression that should make prose seem like the sound of someone talking in a rather low voice into the ear of the person he liked,"[16] and that is precisely what he does in the opening sentence of *The Good Soldier.* "This is the saddest story I have ever heard." As it happens, that's a lie; the story the author is about to narrate is indeed sad, but it is his own; he didn't hear it, he lived it, and now he's here to tell it to you. So he buttonholes the reader in the first line—conversationally, a little seductively—and never lets him go.

A masterpiece like *The Good Soldier* takes such compulsive hold of its audience because the author himself is possessed—by the tale and the people in it, those imaginary

characters with wills of their own, as well as by whatever
obscure needs that drive him on. But before any of that can
begin, he must first be possessed by a voice. Virginia Woolf
put it this way:

> Style is a very simple matter; it is all rhythm. Once you
> get that, you can't use the wrong words. But on the
> other hand here am I sitting half the morning, crammed
> with ideas, and visions, and so on, and can't dislodge
> them, for lack of the right rhythm. Now this is very
> profound, what rhythm is, and goes far deeper than
> words. A sight, an emotion, creates this wave in the
> mind, long before it makes words to fit it; and in writ-
> ing (such is my present belief) one has to recapture this,
> and set this working (which has nothing apparently to
> do with words), and then, as it breaks and tumbles in
> the mind, it makes words to fit it.[17]

The process, as Woolf describes it, may be subtle and
delicate, but it is by no means the monopoly of highbrow
writers. Anita Loos and Elmore Leonard have voices that
are as true and uniquely their own as those of Virginia
Woolf or Mark Twain. Elmore Leonard, whose prose is
unfailingly chaste and economical, has posted on his Web
site ten rules for writing well. All of them are about avoiding high style and fancy writing, about cutting away the
dross and literary pretensions, about constantly simplifying
in order to remain invisible as a writer. At the end, he sums
them up in a single rule: "If it sounds like writing, I
rewrite it."

Style, as I've said, is different from voice, and sometimes

the style you have labored to achieve—your stylishness—
gets in the way of what you have to say. That is certainly
how it was with Plath, who began as a carver and became
a modeler. She sweated over her early poems as if she were
chipping granite and the results are so self-consciously
perfect that they seem evasive, as though perfection were a
way of avoiding what she was really trying to say. All that
changed in the last months of her life, when her demon
had her by the throat and the poems seemed to flow
effortlessly and daily—sometimes as often as three a day.
Yet even in this modeler's dream of creativity, she stayed
true to her carver's training, rewriting obsessionally, until
the poems had achieved their own and very different style
of perfection.

She did so because poets, above all, are driven by the idea
of linguistic perfection. As someone who writes prose for a
living and poems when I get lucky, I assure you that the two
activities are curiously different. No matter how many times
you rewrite prose or how easily it seems to read when you
are done with it, prose is never quite finished. There is
always a word ill-chosen or out of place, a repetition you
missed, an adjective that could be cut, a comma that should
have been a semicolon—something to set your teeth on
edge when you reread it later in cold print. Poems don't
work like that. They are as intricate as the giant locks on a
bank vault: each one of the dozens of tumblers has to click
into place before the door will swing open. A poem, I
mean, isn't finished until every word is precisely weighted
and precisely placed, and if the poet is serious, he knows, to
his sorrow, when he has it wrong and it won't let him rest.

Once he's got it right, however, he knows with equal certainty that there is nothing more to be done; he has produced something that, for the time being, is as near perfect as he can make it. And that is a satisfaction worth sweating for. "In the strange faculty of doing certain things irrelevant to life," wrote Paul Valéry, "with as much care, passion and persistence as if one's life depended on them . . . there we find what is called 'living.'"

I am talking about the craftsman's obsession with detail—obsession in its least pathological form—and in poetry, as in all the arts, that is where the fascination lies. Yeats called it "the fascination of what's difficult," and it has nothing much to do with the trinity of motives— "fame, riches and the love of beautiful women"—which Freud believed spurred artists on. The fascination, as Yeats described it, is with simply getting it right—where "it" is a work with a life of its own, wholly independent of the artist and indifferent to him.

Chapter 2

LISTENING

Movement is the silent music of the body.
—WILLIAM HARVEY

*When the mode of the music changes, the walls
of the city shake.*
—PLATO

No one becomes a real writer without first finding his or her own voice—the one that Philip Roth said "begins at around the back of the knees and reaches well above the head." But finding a voice implies there are readers out there who know how to listen, and listening is a skill almost as tricky as writing. It is even, in its way, an art itself, born out of the same obscure passion that animates every writer—the love of language and what Cheever called "its intimacy, its mysteriousness, its power to evoke." The good reader listens as attentively as the writer writes, hearing the tones and overtones and changes of pitch, as absorbed and alert as if he and the writer were in conversation together. Listening this way is the opposite of speed-reading; it is like reading out loud— but silently and in the head.

Listen, for example, to two variations on a similar theme,

both of which climax with the same triumphant image: first, Yeats's "A Deep-Sworn Vow," published in 1919:

> *Others because you did not keep*
> *That deep-sworn vow have been friends of mine;*
> *Yet always when I look death in the face,*
> *When I clamber to the heights of sleep,*
> *Or when I grow excited with wine,*
> *Suddenly I meet your face.*

Now Cole Porter's variations on a similar theme, written fifteen years later:

> *My story is much too sad to be told,*
> *But practically everything leaves me totally cold.*
> *The only exception I know is the case*
> *Where I'm out on a quiet spree,*
> *Fighting vainly the old ennui,*
> *And I suddenly turn and see*
> *Your fabulous face.*

The words and the music of "I Get a Kick Out of You" are now so hardwired together that I don't think it is possible to read Cole Porter's lyrics without hearing the song. The stunning final image opens the door, as it were, onto the stunning melody, yet the lines that lead up to it are curiously slack and low-key—a chatty recitative, a deliberately nonchalant meander toward revelation, as if the singer were clearing his throat before he bursts into song. Although it's impossible to know, I'm convinced the melody came first, if only because once it kicks in the lyrics become sharp, inventive, and stylish, as though to match it.

Yeats, on the other hand, has to create his own, not quite perceptible music for "A Deep-Sworn Vow," and get it into the poem surreptitiously, without instruments, almost without anyone noticing. How does he do it? Certainly not by traditional prosody: only the third of the six lines is an iambic pentameter with the regulation ten syllables; the first line has eight syllables, the second, fourth, and fifth have nine, the last has a mere seven. This last line literally brings the poem up short with what looks like an abrupt statement of fact but is, in reality, an imaginative leap so startling that in an otherwise carefully rhymed poem Yeats doesn't even bother to look for a new rhyme. He simply repeats the word "face" because that's what the poem is about: her face has haunted him all his life, so when he looks death in the face it is hers that he sees. The effect of this rough music is to create not a melody, like Cole Porter, but a presence—a resigned voice speaking urgently in your ear.

Rough or otherwise, it is ultimately a question of music—or rather, of a musical ear, as Coleridge described it *à propos* the young Shakespeare:

The man that hath not music in his soul can indeed never be a genuine poet. Imagery . . . , affecting incidents, just thoughts, interesting personal or domestic feelings, and with these the art of their combination or intertexture in the form of a poem, may all by incessant effort be acquired as a trade, by a man of talent and much reading, who . . . has mistaken an intense desire of poetic reputation for a natural poetic genius. . . . But the sense of musical delight, with the power of producing it, is a gift of imagination. . . . [It] may be cultivated and improved, but can never be learned.[1]

This ear for the inner music of a line—for the immediacy and disturbance that go to create an authentic voice— is the poetic equivalent of perfect pitch, and, as Coleridge says, it is not the same as a technical mastery of the metrical rules and regulations we call prosody. The latter may "by incessant effort be acquired as a trade, by a man of talent and much reading," but perfect pitch is a natural gift, innate and instinctive, by which the best poets give new life to exhausted conventions and mold them to suit themselves. And this was a concern that was very much on the minds of the Modernist poets a century ago when they turned their backs on traditional forms and began to experiment with free verse.

I want to expand for a moment on the subject of poetry and music. In its beginnings poetry was linked with prophecy and religious ritual and the exalted states of mind they generate. Poets were storytellers, but they were also people inspired, like priests, and they employed a heightened, thickened language as a token of their aroused state, as though to show they meant business. And because the first poems were spoken long before they were written down, the epic poets who wrote *Gilgamesh,* the *Iliad*, and *Beowulf* used the hypnotic qualities of rhythm or rhyme or alliteration both as an *aide-mémoire* for themselves and to catch and hold the audience's attention. This was not an easy task in the days when reading itself was a rare accomplishment. One of the Chaucer manuscripts, for instance, is illuminated with a little picture of the poet reading *Troilus and Criseyde* at a royal banquet: the king and his courtiers are feasting at a long table, busily chatting away, toasting each other, and apparently taking no notice of poor Chaucer, who sits glumly in front of them reading from the manuscript on his knee. The date was late in the fourteenth century, so I imagine the poet of *Beowulf* had had an even harder time in the mead hall four or five hundred years earlier.

In other words, oral poetry was storytelling in a language enriched by quasi-musical tricks that made the audience sit up and listen, and so prevented the poem from becoming just another pleasant background noise, a kind of verbal Muzak. In sophisticated cultures like ancient Athens and Rome and Renaissance Europe, when poets wrote for the elite audience of those who could read, metrical skill became a technical pleasure all of its own and there was a special place on Parnassus for the poet as virtuoso. Hence, in the age of Milton, for example, the brief reverence for Abraham Cowley's unreadable Pindaric odes. Hence, more pertinently, the honorable tradition, which withstood even the Romantic idealization of genius, that no one could be a poet without first being a craftsman, a master of rhyme and meter. In short, poetry was a hard discipline, a skill to be learned, like drawing from life, that stayed with you no matter what you did with it later.

By the end of the nineteenth century, however, when Swinburne's trancelike poems were the model of excellence, metrical virtuosity had almost taken over from meaning.* Modernism was, among other things, a reaction against this sonorous but empty virtuosity, a highbrow revolt against mindlessness. That was what Pound was implying when he said, "Poetry should be at least as well written as prose." His slogan was "Make it new," and one of the keys to making it new was free verse: "to compose," he wrote, "in sequence of the musical phrase, not in sequence of the metronome." I. A. Richards put it better in his influential *Principles of Literary Criticism*, which was written—in 1924—in part to help validate T. S. Eliot's baffling new poetry:

> The whole conception of metre as "*uniformity* in variety," a kind of mental drill in which words, those erratic and varied things, do their best to behave as though they were all the same, with certain concessions, licenses and equivalences allowed, should nowadays be obsolete.[2]

Richards called rhythm a "texture of expectations, satisfactions, disappointments, surprisals, which the sequence of syllables brings about," and what he says about listening with fresh ears sounds very like Hulme, in the passage I quoted earlier, on the need to see with fresh eyes:

* In Longfellow's "Hiawatha," the hypnotic meter throbs along under its own steam, almost impervious to meaning, as illustrated in the parody "Hiawatha's Gloves": "He, to get the cold side outside, / Put the warm side, fur side, inside. / He, to get the warm side inside, / Put the cold side, skin side, outside . . . ," etc.

Freshness convinces you, you feel at once that the artist is in an actual physical state. You feel that for a minute. Real communication is so very rare, for plain speech is unconvincing. It is in this rare fact of communication that you get the root of aesthetic pleasure.

I shall maintain that wherever you get an extraordinary interest in a thing, great zest in its contemplation which carries on the contemplator to accurate description . . . , there you have sufficient justification for poetry. It must be an intense zest which heightens a thing out of the level of prose.[3]

Hulme was the original Imagist and he was talking about images, about what happens when a poet, concentrating on some scene or object, describes it precisely as he sees it, fresh-minted, and without reference to conventional ways of looking. But when Hulme says, "Freshness convinces you, you feel at once that the artist is in an actual physical state," what he is describing has, I think, as much to do with music and rhythm as with visual imagery.

As I have written elsewhere,[4] someone once said that rhythm is the one thing a poet can never fake. He was talking about inner rhythm, the natural breath of a line, which has very little to do with regular prosody, with the mechanical thumpity-thump of traditionally polished verse:

The Assyrian came down like the wolf on the fold,
And his cohorts were gleaming in silver and gold.

That is poetry of the metronome; you know in advance precisely where every stress will fall. Now listen to a couple of lines from the garden scene near the end of *The Merchant of Venice*:

Peace, ho! The moon sleeps with Endymion
And would not be awaked.

All Portia means is, "Look, they're necking!," but the way she says it is as unquiet and alerting as the sound of flowing water. The first line is an iambic pentameter, but prosody is a clumsy instrument and if, God forbid, you wanted a technical analysis of how the lines work, you would probably do better to use chaos theory, the science of nonlinear, dynamic systems—such as, indeed, that of running water—in which the parts act on each other in imperceptible ways to produce complex and unpredictable behavior.

This is just a highfalutin way of describing what good poetry does: feelings—not the grand emotions aspired to, but the altogether subtler sense of being emotionally awakened—are expressed less in imagery than in movement, in the inner rhythm of the language. When a poet is genuinely aroused, you can hear it in the way the lines move. And when the rhythm is dead, no amount of invention can disguise the fact. In this respect, poetry and music are similar: the rhythm—the way the sounds combine, separate, recombine—is the vehicle for the feeling. I know from my own experience as a poet that it is sometimes possible to hear a poem before you know what it is about, to get the movement before you get the words, as though the movement were a dimly heard wake-up call or the first

faint stirring of something waiting to be expressed. And
without that inner movement or disturbance, the words,
no matter how fetching, remain inert. The line itself may
contain no visual elements at all—Coleridge's "And the
spring comes slowly up this way"—or the imagery may be
suppressed and at a remove—Sir Thomas Wyatt's "Busily
seeking with a continual change"—but if you listen properly, you can hear it stir and pause and breathe.

Listen, for example, to the opening of D. H. Lawrence's
"Snake," which is seemingly in free verse:

> *A snake came to my water-trough*
> *On a hot, hot day, and I in pyjamas for the heat,*
> *To drink there.*
>
> *In the deep, strange-scented shade of the great dark carob-tree*
> *I came down the steps with my pitcher*
> *And must wait, must stand and wait, for there he was at the*
>   *trough before me.*

What you have here are two totally different states of
mind—inner and outer, matter-of-fact and aroused—and
they alternate with each other. In the first stanza, lines 1
and 3 combine to make a flat statement of fact—"A snake
came to my water-trough to drink there"—which is
interrupted by the stirrings of something expectant and
strange: "On a hot, hot day, and I in pyjamas for the heat."
In the second stanza, the strangeness has begun to take
over and the straight narrative is confined to the middle
line—"I came down the steps with my pitcher." All this is

done implicitly: the poet doesn't talk about what he's feeling; he implies it by the disturbance of the lines themselves. In Lawrence's own words, they "make me prick my innermost ear."

John Donne had a genius for opening lines that make his readers sit up and attend: "I wonder, by my troth, what thou and I / Did, till we loved?"; "By our first strange and fatal interview"; "Twice or thrice had I loved thee, / Before I knew thy face or name"; "Death be not proud"; and so on. But it is not simply his now-hear-this authority that stops you in your tracks. He also writes in such a way as to make you feel that you are face-to-face with him. Barbara Everett was responding to this uncanny, almost physical immediacy when she wrote, "Whenever I open Donne, on a good reading day, I am struck by an extraordinary distinction and strength and originality of mind and gift. Donne is so generously, even unnervingly present on the page."[5] In a poem called "The Blossom," Donne spoke of "my naked, thinking heart," and that seems to describe exactly what he expresses in his best poems: you can hear his heart beat *and* you can hear him think, as though they were one and the same process.

Maybe that is always what they are at a truly creative level, and not just in the arts. This is how Albert Einstein described the preverbal way ideas came to him as a physicist:

Words or language, as they are written or spoken, do not seem to play any role in my mechanism of thought. The psychical entities which seem to serve as elements of thought are certain signs and more or less clear images

which can be "voluntarily" reproduced and combined. . . .
The above mentioned elements are, in my case, of visual
and some muscular type. Conventional words or other
signs have to be sought for laboriously only in a second
stage, when the mentioned associative play is sufficiently
established and can be reproduced at will.[6]

Mind and body are indivisible, Einstein is implying, and
creative thinking is a physical process, "visual and . . . muscular," deeply embedded in the body-mind.

Three centuries earlier, Donne had said much the same,
and also demonstrated the idea by the way in which he
expressed it:

> *we understood*
> *Her by her sight; her pure and eloquent blood*
> *Spoke in her cheeks, and so distinctly wrought,*
> *That one might almost say, her body thought.*

Note how the rhythm echoes and intensifies what he is
saying: the line breaks stress the key words, "understood"
and "spoke"; the pausing hesitant movement of "That one
might almost say, her body thought" seems to imitate the
process of thinking—first you cast around, then you
pounce. According to Schopenhauer, "Thoughts die the
moment they are embodied by words." Not in this
instance. As Donne describes it, thinking is as physical and
dramatic as dancing.

That is how it always seems to be in creative writing. At
the end of his poem "Among Schoolchildren," Yeats asks,

"How can we know the dancer from the dance?" He is talking about knowledge and the indivisibility of idea and form. In those terms, poetry is like dance: it has a bodily dimension, a kind of muscular depth that moves both the poet and the reader in ways they are not quite aware of.

Music, too, works in a similar way. The listener hears a piece of music as a process, as an extended, intricate conversation between instruments. But for this conversation to take place and make sense, the musicians have to think vertically as well as horizontally—in chords and harmonies as well as in phrases. Musicians themselves take this for granted: "There are many ways of balancing a chord," Alfred Brendel has said, "and one must eventually learn to measure the sound of a chord in one's imagination and then control it in performance." The quotation is from *The Veil of Order*, a series of conversations between Brendel and the critic Michael Meyer. The book takes its title from an aphorism of Novalis: "Chaos, in a work of art, should shimmer through the veil of order." This is an idea that appeals strongly to Brendel: "I am very much for chaos, that is to say feeling. But it's only the veil of order that makes the work of art possible."[7] He seems to be implying that feeling, the chaos that wells up vertically from the unconscious, is made orderly by the horizontal phrasing and development, but without the chaos of feeling there can be no music. It is the same with language: argument, meter, and tone of voice create order, but everything depends on the weight and resonance of each word.

In the *Four Quartets* Eliot writes of "music heard so deeply / That it is not heard at all, but you are the music /

While the music lasts." Poems, too, take possession of the
reader, though in a different way: not by abstracting the
self from the self but by a curiously physical arousal. "All
poetry is an affair of the body," Hulme wrote, "—that is, to
be read it must affect the body."[8] I. A. Richards thought
the same:

> We must not think of [metre] as in the words them-
> selves or in the thumping of a drum. It is not in the
> stimulation, it is in our response. Metre adds to all the
> variously fated expectancies which make up rhythm a
> definite temporal pattern and its effect is not due to our
> perceiving a pattern in something outside us, but to our
> becoming patterned ourselves. With every beat of the
> metre a tide of anticipation in us turns and swings, set-
> ting up as it does so extraordinarily sympathetic rever-
> berations. We shall never understand metre so long as
> we ask, "Why does temporal pattern so excite us?" and
> fail to realise that the pattern itself is a vast cyclic agita-
> tion spreading all over the body, a tide of excitement
> pouring through the channels of the mind."[9]

For the poet who produces this tide of excitement, inner
rhythm is the poetic equivalent of body language, and style
itself, as the Australian poet Les Murray describes it, has
deep physical roots:

> You've got to be able to dream at the same time as you
> think to write poetry. You think with a double mind. It's
> like thinking with both sides of your brain at once. And if
> you can't do that, you can't write poetry. You can write

expository prose, but poetry is as much dreamed as it is thought and it is as much danced in the body as it is written. It's done in your lungs. It's done in every part of your muscles—you can feel it in your muscles."[10]

Les Murray is an unusually physical poet, not just in his apprehension of the world and the way he writes about it, but also in himself. He is a powerful man with a voracious appetite and prone to obesity (he eats when he is depressed; during one particularly acute and extended period of depression his weight went up to an astonishing 350 pounds). But I think the physicality he is talking about is all in the mind: it is an appetite for places and people, for the sheer diversity of the physical world and the rich taste of words in his mouth.

There is, of course, no necessary or obvious correlation between an artist's physique and his work, although Hemingway clearly thought otherwise. That chaste and close-mouthed style of his may have degenerated into a macho pose, but not until later when he was famous and indulged and getting flabby. When he was starting out—a young man who fished and hunted and boxed as well as wrote—he honed his prose as rigorously as an athlete in training hones his body in order to create, as it were, the literary equivalent of an athlete's physical purity and asceticism.

Perhaps this is what Roland Barthes meant when he wrote:

Imagery, delivery, vocabulary spring from the body and the past of the writer and gradually become the very reflexes of his art. Thus under the name of style a self-sufficient language is evolved which has its roots only in the depths of the author's personal and secret mythology. . . . Its frame of reference is biological or biographical, not historical.[11]

Barthes seems to be saying that an author's style is an expression of his unique physical existence in the world, an idea that is particularly appropriate to Hemingway and his prose. For other artists, however, this fit between style and physique is anything but smooth and predictable, and sometimes the creator and the work seem irredeemably at odds. Debussy, for example: his music is delicate, atmospheric, attenuated, ethereal, but the man himself, according to a contemporary, looked like a radish—earthy, round, fiery, and full of appetite.

Poetry, as Les Murray describes it, has to be simultaneously dreamed and felt in the body. But then, dreaming itself is already a kind of physical thinking. It takes place in REM sleep when the body is shut down, the muscles are paralyzed, and only the eyes move. Meanwhile, the mind goes on working, though in a different way: it expresses its thoughts not abstractly in words but concretely in images and dramatically in gestures, as in a charade. And that, I suggest, is how language works in a poem. Henry James described the creative imagination as the "deep well of unconscious cerebration." The thoughts and images and plots that emerge from this well are not simply drenched in the artist's unconscious, they are also thick with a kind of physical residue. This fusing together of mind and body is what I mean when I talk about the artist's voice and presence.

It is an idea that applies particularly to Shakespeare. He was writing at a time when the English language had not yet settled down—its rules were vague, its meanings not yet fixed*—and one aspect of his genius was the way he extended its possibilities. In the great, twenty-volume *Oxford English Dictionary* an astonishing number of first usages are ascribed to him. This happens especially in his later plays when he seems to be feeling his way toward a thought in the process of thinking it and the complexity of what he is saying pushes him toward the limits of language. This process culminates in *King Lear*, where something strange happens to his language, as though he were going beyond mere words into some more visceral form of apprehension.

Lear is the greatest of his plays but also the cruelest, bleakest, and most unrelentingly pessimistic. (In all the other versions of the story, Cordelia survives to provide some semblance of a happy ending. Not in Shakespeare's.) "In *Lear*," Frank Kermode writes in a fine essay, "there is a way of looking at people as if they were simply basic human beings, naturally naked, wretches whose standing as more than that depends on their additions, without which they might be indistinguishable from Poor Tom: 'unaccommodated man is no more but such a poor, bare, fork'd

---

* I think modern American-English is similarly malleable and open to the vernacular, which may be why the best twentieth-century American writers often seemed more linguistically energetic than their British counterparts.

animal . . . ' "[12] "Additions" is Shakespeare's word for those material and moral refinements that make for civilization—wealth, clothing, shelter, honors, kindness, gratitude, loyalty and, above all, the bonds between children and their parents. These are the fragile defenses society has built to keep out chaos, and without them, in Albany's words, "It will come, / Humanity must perforce prey upon itself, / Like monsters of the deep."

This is precisely what happens in *Lear*. The king begins by willfully stripping himself of his kingdom and then is unwillingly stripped of everything else—his retinue, his robes, his sanity.* And steadily throughout the play, as if to mirror the relentless nihilism of the action, Shakespeare, too, is stripping his language of embellishments and "additions" until he is left, at the close, with the bare roots, Anglo-Saxon and monosyllabic: "I know when one is dead and when one lives; / She's dead as earth." As for Lear's last desolate cry:

> *Why should a dog, a horse, a rat have life,*
> *And thou no breath at all? Thou'lt come no more,*
> *Never, never, never, never, never.*

In these linguistically reduced circumstances, the two syllables of "never" resound like a grand rhetorical device.

"Nihilism" is too mild and restricted a word for *King*

---

* This exercise in nihilism is echoed in the dialogue. In the opening act, the most often repeated word is "nothing": "*Cordelia*: Nothing, my lord. *Lear*: Nothing? *Cordelia*: Nothing. *Lear*: Nothing will come of nothing. Speak again." And so on. The Fool later takes the word up and runs it into the ground.

Lear. Shakespeare is portraying an unredeemed Hobbesian world, and he is exploring it at its most elemental level, deeper and bleaker than the Oedipus complex, and far beyond the pleasure principle, as if the bond between parent and child were more primal than the primal scene— perhaps because, as Shakespeare saw it, it echoes the bond between the Creator and his creation. This is not a level that can easily be reached or apprehended or expressed, and in order to get close to it Shakespeare strips his language of all "additions" until it becomes in itself a linguistic mirror of Doomsday, "the promised end," an "image of that horror" as naked and as cruel as the Last Judgment itself.

The usual rules don't apply to a genius like Shakespeare, who could do anything and get away with it, so I want to give a more straightforward example of how the shift in our attitude to meter and our awareness of inner rhythm can change the way we read a poem.

Andrew Marvell and Sir Thomas Wyatt both translated the second chorus from Seneca's tragedy, *Thyestes.* This is Marvell's version:

> *Climb at* Court *for me that will*
> *Tottering Favour's slipp'ry hill.*
> *All I seek is to lye still.*
> *Settled in some secret Nest*
> *In calm Leisure let me rest;*
> *And far off the publick Stage*
> *Pass away my silent Age.*
> *Thus when without noise, unknown,*
> *I have liv'd out all my span,*

I shall dye, without a groan,
An old honest Country man.
Who expos'd to others Eyes,
Into his own Heart ne'r pry's,
Death to him's a Strange surprise.

Marvell was a famously accomplished Classicist, and his version of Seneca is appropriately smooth and sonorous. He was also a man of great fastidiousness who had removed himself from London and the turmoil of the civil war and was living a secluded pastoral life at Nun Appleton House in deepest Yorkshire, tutoring the daughter of his patron General Fairfax, while Oliver Cromwell was off slaughtering the Scots and Irish. As it happens, Marvell's disdain for politics didn't last; he was soon to land a government job—he joined his friend Milton as Latin Secretary to the Council of State—then became a Member of Parliament, renowned for his fierce political satires and pamphlets, which was how he was remembered until his lyric poems were rediscovered almost three centuries later. For the time being, however, he was resolutely above the fray, and I think you can hear this in his cozy vision of himself "settled in some secret nest / In calm leisure . . . An old honest Country man." His translation is a masterly exercise in poetic technique—the lines run like silk between his fingers—but the tone of voice is unwaveringly complacent.

Compare that to Wyatt's version of the poem:

Stand who so list upon the Slipper top
Of courts' estates, and let me hear rejoice;

And use me quiet without let or stop,
Unknown in court, that hath such brackish joys.
In hidden place, so let my days forth pass,
That when my years be done, withouten noise,
I may die aged after the common trace.
For him death gripeth right hard by the crop
That is much known of others; and of himself, alas,
Doth die unknown, dazed with dreadful face.

Wyatt's translation was written a century or so before Marvell's, and it is neither sonorous nor cozy. Marvell and his contemporaries would have thought it barbarous, and even Elizabethan poets, who honored Wyatt for introducing them to Petrarch and the sonnet, had difficulty making his poems scan and were bothered by the roughness of his rhymes and rhythms. They preferred the metrically smoother and more sweetly chiming verse of his duller contemporary, the Earl of Surrey.

From a modern point of view, however, the awkwardness is part of the poem's power and authority. Unlike Marvell, Wyatt was not above the fray; he was deeply immersed in the tangled politics of Henry VIII's court and a powerful figure in it—Ambassador to Spain, special envoy to France, Marshal of Calais, Sheriff of Kent, Member of Parliament, and Vice-Admiral elect of the Fleet. Being close to King Henry was a risky business—Wyatt himself was twice imprisoned on trumped-up charges—and it also meant watching friends die. He was present at the execution of his patron, Thomas Cromwell, and he was also present—watching, it is said, from a room above the gate of the

Tower of London—when Anne Boleyn was beheaded, along
with several of her supposed lovers. Wyatt himself had been
Anne's lover before she married the king, and he would
surely have gone to the scaffold with her if he hadn't
warned Henry that she was not a suitable wife.

Taking all this into account, listen again to how the two
poets deal with Seneca's closing lines on death and self-
knowledge: *illi mors gravis incubat / qui notus nimis omnibus /
ignotus moritur sibi*: "Death falls heavy on the man / who,
known too much by the world, / dies unknown to himself." In Marvell's lilting version this becomes:

> *Who expos'd to others Eyes,*
> *Into his own Heart ne'r pry's,*
> *Death to him's a Strange surprise.*

That is accurate and economical, but so far removed from
the horrors of death and final things, as well as from the
gravity of Seneca's meter, that it seems positively light-
hearted. Compare that with Wyatt:

> *For him death gripeth right hard by the crop*
> *That is much known of others; and of himself, alas,*
> *Doth die unknown, dazed with dreadful face.*

The fierce imagery is made fiercer by the jolting rhythm
and sibilant half-rhyme. Death, for Wyatt, is a violent physical presence that grabs its victim by the neck and thrusts
its face close. Hence, the shocking ambiguity of that last
phrase, "dazed with dreadful face": Is the dying man dazed

with surprise because he is unprepared or dazed by the violence of it all? Is his face full of dread or is the face of his executioner dreadful? Alas, indeed. The poem may only have been yet another translation of a much-translated Renaissance favorite, but the topic was one that Wyatt knew from the inside, so—just as he had done with his marvelous free translation of Petrarch's sonnet, "Whoso list to hunt"—he highjacked the original and re-created it for his own ends in his own troubled voice.

I am not suggesting that Wyatt's version is superior to Marvell's because Wyatt, the courtier, knew what he was talking about, while Marvell, still years away from a political career, was translating Seneca primarily as a literary exercise. The difference, instead, is in the way the two poets read the original and filtered it through their differing sensibilities—for Wyatt, the poem is about the deadly perils of fame and politics; for Marvell, it is a comfortable tribute to anonymity and rural seclusion—and the sources of that difference have less to do with biographical facts than with literary presence, with the unique way in which, to rephrase Barthes, a writer's style expresses his character, history, and even his physiology. Being present on the page, I mean, matters far more than having been present at whatever it is you are describing.

The New Critics took for granted that the divorce between the creator and the created was absolute. For them, the "Intentional Fallacy"—interpreting a work in terms of its author's biography or psychology—was one of the two greatest crimes against literature. (The other was the "Affective Fallacy"—interpreting it subjectively in terms of its mysterious, unquantifiable effects on the reader's emotions.) Half a century later, the compass has swung firmly in the opposite direction: it is now so unusual to discuss a work of art without talking about the writer's life that literature itself seems in danger of being upstaged by biography. For lazy readers, biography is a shortcut, as a way of knowing everything you need to know about an author without the bother of laboring through the collected works. Others, more serious, are intrigued by the creative process and assume that people who write are as fascinating as the work they produce.

Unfortunately, there is no necessary connection between the interesting world a writer creates in the reader's head and the facts of the writer's life, not least because writing is a sedentary middle-class profession, too time-consuming to leave much opportunity for an interesting life. Some authors, like Joseph Conrad, lead interesting lives in their youth, then settle down and write about them later, but most, like oysters, need only minor irritants to get them going.

There are also some writers for whom writing is a charm against an intolerable reality, and for them the differences between the lived facts and the imagined story are greatest when the two are almost identical. Jean Rhys, for example, had artistic imagination and no invention at all: she couldn't dream up situations she herself had not been in, the people in her stories were the people she knew, and a great deal of what she wrote in her diaries she rewrote in

her novels. But the style of her writing—offhand yet puri-
fied and austere—was utterly at odds with the interesting
but desperate life she had been doomed to.

By the time she started writing, Rhys was in her thirties
and had already been a chorus girl, a mannequin, a rich
man's mistress, and a part-time prostitute. She had also
become a chronic alcoholic and drink turned her into a
monster—violent, vengeful, foul-mouthed, manipulative,
and blankly indifferent to husbands, lovers, children, and
friends. Like Rhys, the heroines in most of her novels are
on a kamikaze mission to drink themselves to death, but
she redeemed their squalid lives by transforming them into
high art, distilling them in a chaste and delicate prose, and
telling their stories in a tone of voice that is casual, clear,
self-denying, and disabused. This, for example, from *Good
Morning, Midnight*, is how she describes the death of her
three-week-old son in a Paris hospital for the poor:

> I can't feed this unfortunate baby. He is taken out and
> given Nestlés milk. So, I can sleep. . . .

> The next day [the midwife] comes in and says: "Now I
> am going to arrange that you will be just like what you
> were before. There will be no trace, no mark, nothing."
>   That, it seems, is her solution.
>   She swathes me up in very tight, very uncomfortable
> bandages. Intricately she rolls them and ties them. She
> gives me to understand that this is usually an extra. She
> charges a great deal for this as a rule.
>   "I do this better than anyone in the whole of Paris,"

she says. "Better than any doctor, better than any of these people who advertise, better than anyone in the whole of Paris."

And there I lie in these damned bandages for a week. And there he lies, swathed up too, like a little mummy. And never crying.

But now I like taking him in my arms and looking at him. A lovely forehead, incredibly white, the eyebrows drawn very faintly in gold dust. . . .

Well, this was a funny time. (The big bowl of coffee in the morning with a pattern of red and blue flowers. I was always so thirsty.) But uneasy, uneasy. . . . Ought a baby to be as pretty as this, as pale as this, as silent as this? The other babies yell from morning to night. Uneasy. . . .

When I complain about the bandages she says: "I promise you that when you take them off you'll be just as you were before." And it is true. When she takes them off there is not one line, not one wrinkle, not one crease.

And five weeks afterwards there I am, with not one line, not one wrinkle, not one crease.

And there he is, lying with a ticket tied round his wrist because he died in a hospital. And there I am looking down at him, without one line, without one wrinkle, without one crease. . . .

In the novel, the mother's vanity and the way the midwife plays along with it are part of a terrible irony. The reality, as described in Carole Angier's biography of Rhys, was just as terrible but altogether shabbier. The baby died because of Rhys's profound incompetence and even profounder indifference. She had left him in his cot by an open window on a bitter January day and he developed pneumonia; the parents took their time before they called the *sage femme* who called a doctor; while the baby was dying in the Hospice des Enfants Assistés, Rhys and her feckless husband were getting giggly drunk on champagne, trying to pretend the disaster wasn't happening.

The voice in the novel is that of the woman Rhys herself might have wished to have been if booze, penury, and disappointment hadn't destroyed her. And that, I think, is the impulse behind all her work: she tended her writing as meticulously as she tended her looks, distilling and reshaping the facts to make them seem inevitable, in the hope that her restrained and delicate prose might redeem her shameful life and transform it into something beautiful. "All of a writer that matters is in the book or books," she once wrote. "It is idiotic to be curious about the person." No doubt Carole Angier was right when she said that Rhys refused to authorize a biography because "she had too much to hide." But as Rhys saw it, any biography, however sympathetic and scrupulous, would have been a betrayal of everything she had put into her art.

"You never want facts to get in the way of truth," said the novelist Robert Stone, whose youth was almost as adventurous as Conrad's and a good deal more unruly. "That's why fiction is more satisfying than non-fiction." Lying, that is, is part of the creative writers' trade: they take what they know, twist it to suit themselves, then blame the outcome on imagination. But the one area in which the genuine writer never lies is in the art of writing itself, the laborious, unforgiving, sorry business—Beckett's word for it was "balls-aching"—of putting words down on paper precisely and with restraint. As I suggested in the first chapter, it is a craft, like a carpenter's or a stonemason's, that has little to do with the writer's public personality or even his private image of himself. Instead, it has to do with "it," the impersonal work itself whose rigorous demands you are trying to satisfy for no other reason than the dubious pleasure of getting it right.

Jean Rhys was so obsessed with getting it right that she wrote and rewrote her novels, over and over, unwilling to let them go with the slightest blemish on them, perhaps in the belief that only by producing something flawless could she justify the otherwise unjustifiable mess she had made of her life. But the style of perfection she was after belongs to poetry and is not easily achieved in the "loose, baggy monster" that is the novel. As I said before, one of the pleasures of writing a poem is at least you know when you've got it right—or as right as you are ever going to get it—because, even in free verse, a poem isn't finished until each word is locked in its right place. Yet paradoxically, this concentration, where every word bears its own weight and has its own resonance, creates in itself its own special kind of freedom. Consider, for example, the opening of Richard Lovelace's fifteen-line masterpiece, "La Bella Bona Roba":

I cannot tell who loves the skeleton
Of a poor marmoset, naught but bone, bone.
Give me a nakedness with her clothes on.

Such whose white satin upper coat of skin,
Cut upon velvet, rich incarnadin,
Hath yet a body and of flesh within . . .

Lovelace was a charming and polished Cavalier poet, a courtly graduate of the school of John Donne, and the poem is a typically elaborate Metaphysical conceit—or rather, a conceit about a conceit. "Bona Roba" was slang for "whore," and Lovelace's conceit was to take the image literally: a whore may wear beautiful clothes, but the truly beautiful dress is her ample body itself, the white satin skin over red velvet flesh. What he saying is simple—he likes fat women—but the way he says it makes his reasons seem not quite as casual and carnal as he would appear. He likes his women fat because with skinny women—"marmoset," little monkey, was also a term of endearment—he can feel the skeleton beneath the skin and it reminds him of his mortality. In the seventeenth century, when "die" had the same erotic connotations as "come" has now, there was nothing unusual about confusing sex and death, but at the court of King Charles it may have been against a gentleman's code to admit to feeling queasy about it. So Lovelace writes a cynical variation on the theme and saves face by letting his uneasiness leak out around the edges, as it were, by playing disturbed variations on the regular iambic pentameters and the single rhyme: he starts brood-

ing and ominous, increases the sense of menace by repeat-
ing the not-quite-perfect rhyme—skeleton/bone, bone—
then cuts himself short with a rapped-out command and a
throwaway rhyme: "Give me a nakedness with her clothes
on." The result is a whole world of unease implied in three
brilliant lines by little more than subtle shifts in tone of
voice and speed of delivery.

The death of the baby in *Good Morning, Midnight* also
compresses great ambiguity into a relatively small space
and depends almost entirely on tone and pace, but Rhys
creates her particular poetry without the safety net of a
poetic form. The passage, of course, isn't poetical in the
Grand Opera manner of "fine writing" and "rich prose."
On the contrary, the tone of voice is steadily conversa-
tional and Rhys is literally playing it by ear. She repeats
simple phrases until they acquire an altogether darker resonance—"without one line, without one wrinkle, without
one crease" starts reassuring and a little boastful and ends
as a denunciation—and she varies pitch and speed, setting
offhand comments and fragments of straight narrative—
"Well, this was a funny time," "The other babies yell from
morning to night"—against a continually anxious, inward
brooding—"uneasy, uneasy." Rhys's genius in this piece of
writing was to describe heartbreak without quite men-
tioning it, to make of it a kind of shorthand—spare, precise, ironic, "without one wrinkle, without one crease,"
and also without a trace of self-pity. Hulme called prose "a
museum where all the old weapons of poetry [are] kept."
But not in this case.

"I have no imagination," Isaac Babel told his friend

Konstantin Paustovsky. "I can't invent. I have to know everything, down to the last vein, otherwise I can't write a thing. My motto is *authenticity*." What he meant by "authenticity" was not, I think, truth to the facts but truth to what his imagination made of the facts in the process of re-creating them in his own voice.

Maybe this is just a roundabout variant of the old truism that artists lie but their art doesn't. As Lawrence said, "Never trust the artist, trust the tale." Sometimes outrageous lies are just what you want as a reader—a blockbuster fantasy to get you through a long flight or a sleepless night. But blockbusters are like action movies with a computer-generated cast—wild fantasies in leaden prose that you read diagonally for the plot, while skipping the descriptive bits and rhetorical flourishes. Authenticity is something else entirely, and, as I said, it is not for skimming because it reveals itself in details the eye doesn't easily take in—in some unexpected hesitation or cunning adverb or barely audible inflection that makes you sit up and take notice. These are the small gestures with which writers announce their presence, and, unlike good children, they must be heard, not seen. The truth is in the voice, and only by tuning into it will you know whether or not you are being conned.

Chapter 3

THE CULT OF PERSONALITY AND THE MYTH OF THE ARTIST

*Do not imagine you can exorcise what oppresses you in life
by giving vent to it in art.*
—FLAUBERT

*All the grief of this century has come from trying to turn life
into art. Think about it.*
—ROBERT STONE

i

I have been talking so far about two of the three R's: the writer's patient, exacting quest for a distinctive voice of his own, and the reader's equally exacting obligation to listen while he reads. Both writing and reading, in the intensive way I've described, are private, inward experiences that take place, like thinking, in silence. In order to write a poem or even an authentic sentence, and to hear it properly, you have to read it out loud silently in your head. But once the poem or the piece of prose is finished, it is sent out into the world to find an audience. This is where the third R comes in—the arithmetic of sales and the razzmatazz it generates in order to turn a writer into a marketable personality—and its effects, in the last few decades, have become increasingly confusing.

There is also a fourth R in the equation, Romanticism and its legacy, and to describe its effect, I want to start with a fragment of partial and potted literary history. Romanticism was a sudden, violent explosion of emotion, enthusiasm, and introspection that erupted in the second half of the eighteenth century, destroying the classical belief in order, reason, symmetry, and calm and clearing the ground for the cult of personality by redefining the concept of genius. Genius in the modern sense, as defined by the *Oxford English Dictionary*—"instinctive and extraordinary capacity for imaginative creation, original thought, invention, or discovery"—is an innovation of the late eighteenth century and it is not in Dr. Johnson's dictionary. Alexander Pope may have been acknowledged as Augustan England's most gifted poet, but he was admired, above all, for the brilliance with which he refined and perfected classical forms, and his patrons regarded him, as the Esterházys regarded Haydn, as little more than an exalted servant. Although Pope was touchy, vengeful, and not famous for his modesty, he believed, like all the Augustans, that "whatever is, is right," including the way society was ordered; when he talked about the World (usually with a capital "W"), he meant the bewigged and corseted beau monde, and he accepted his place in it. For Romantics like Shelley, the world meant untamed nature with a quivering sensibility at its center, and poets were "unacknowledged legislators" whose artistic freedom was part of the larger political movement toward liberty, equality, and fraternity that was shaking society. Like the French Revolution, Romanticism was founded on an idea of freedom—the freedom to feel, react, and create in a personal and unpredictable way—and it involved a profound shift of focus— away from established Augustan certainties and toward subjective experience. Genius as we now understand it is a wholly Romantic concept: not just a great artist, but a great artist who has embarked on an inner journey and makes his own rules as he goes—Beethoven rather than Haydn, Rousseau rather than Dr. Johnson, Rimbaud rather than Pope.

That revolutionary fervor seeped away during the nineteenth century, along with the creative energy and technical innovation it inspired, until Wordsworth's sense of "Bliss was it in that dawn to be alive," expressed in what he called "the real language of men in a state of vivid sensation," had degenerated into empty mellifluousness and Victorian self-righteousness. It was the latter, above all, the relentless moral superiority of their elders that most exasperated the new generation of writers at the turn of the century. Hence, George Moore's tetchy comment on the last stanza of an otherwise innocent and rather beautiful nature lyric by Tennyson:

> *O love, they die in yon rich sky,*
>   *They faint on hill or field or river;*
> *Our echoes roll from soul to soul,*
>   *And grow forever and forever.*

"The Victorian could never reconcile himself to finishing a poem without speaking about the soul, and the lines are particularly vindictive."[1]

During the experimental heyday of the Modernist movement, in the first decades of the twentieth century, "advanced" literary people took for granted that Romanticism was dead and their experiments were not only burying it, but also inaugurating a new period of Classicism. T. E. Hulme's brilliant essay on the theme became one of the key texts of Modernism and influenced T. S. Eliot so profoundly that, as I mentioned earlier, he called Hulme "the forerunner of a new attitude of mind, which should be called the twentieth century mind." Hulme dismissed Romanticism as "spilt religion" because it yearned for the infinite, wallowed in emotion, distrusted the intellect, and paid rather cursory attention to detail. Classicism was the opposite of all that; it implied, among other things, impersonality, intelligence, lucidity, control. In other words, Modernism was an impatient reaction against Romantic self-indulgence and mindlessness; the artists were surfeited with wine and roses and atmosphere; it was time for an altogether more strenuous and unforgiving style.

Just how powerful and reasonable their case was becomes clear if you compare a poem by, say, Swinburne—full of verbal color and rhythmic excitement, but with little to say and vague as to how the pieces fit together—with the deliberately fragmented and allusive style of *The Waste Land*, where a great deal is implied and very little stated outright. It becomes even more powerful if you compare Swinburne's poetry with Eliot's notes to *The Waste Land*, which was where the real polemics were. They implied that the readers should have read not just the classics in several languages but also books that had no obvious connection with poetry, like Frazer's *Golden Bough*, F. H. Bradley's *Appearance and Reality*, Jesse Weston's *From Ritual to Romance*, and the *Handbook of Birds of Eastern North America*; they should be able to work out references, follow an argument, and leap semantic gaps. (My own belief is that the notes were a smokescreen; if you read the poem itself, you get an utterly different impression: that of a precise, delicate and not particularly defended portrait of a man having a nervous breakdown; the notes were a way of confusing the issue.)

By adding footnotes to *The Waste Land*, Eliot was not simply padding out a relatively short poem into something that could be published as a book, he was also defining his audience. Like Donne, whose reputation he did so much to reestablish after almost three centuries of neglect, Eliot was writing for what Elizabethans called "understanders," a select group of people as well educated and intellectual as himself who could pick up the allusions, make the connections, and work out the argument without having them explained. Even Dr. Johnson, who disliked the Metaphysicals, had admitted, "To write on their plan, it was at least necessary to read and think." Eliot rephrased that in twentieth-century terms: "A thought to Donne was an experience; it modified his sensibility." Later, when the Romantic aversion to thinking seemed to have been disposed of, he summed up his position more bluntly in a throwaway remark *à propos* of some philosopher's inept discussion of Aristotle's "method": "The only method," he said, wearily and in parentheses, "is to be very intelligent."

Romanticism took longer to die in the universities, which was not surprising considering that at Oxford, when I was a student there half a century ago, the English syllabus ended around 1830; everything after that date was thought to be modern and therefore not worthy of scholarly attention. In those days, English departments were small and generally looked down on by the other faculties. English was like geography and forestry, a subject you read if you weren't up to tackling a serious discipline like classics or mathematics or the sciences. Oddly enough, the English faculty thought the same and, in the name of intellectual rigor, forced us to spend a third of our time—three out of the nine papers in the final examinations—studying Old English, Middle English, and modern philology. So far as Oxford was concerned, philology and scholarship were the only ways in which this down-market subject could acquire a little academic prestige.

The New Criticism was, among other things, a reaction against this snobbish conviction that the study of literature was an easy option. It had developed in response to Modernism and what Yeats called "the fascination with what's difficult," flourished in highbrow quarterly reviews, and was founded on the belief that being sensitive to literature wasn't necessarily at odds with being intelligent. "Our policy," wrote the editors of the *Partisan Review,* William Phillips and Philip Rahv, "has been to resist the growing division in modern culture between the sensibility of art and the more rational intelligence that has gone into social and philosophical thinking."[2] In other words, it was possible to be shaken by a poem, then think about why you were shaken and give your reasons, instead of merely throwing up your hands in wonder, as the impressionist critics did, then trying to upstage the thing with your own gaudy prose. William Empson put it most eloquently: "Critics as 'barking dogs' . . . are of two sorts: those who merely relieve themselves against the flower of beauty, and those, less continent, who afterwards scratch it up."[3] Repeat "afterwards": first you reacted, then you gave your reasons for reacting by analyzing what it was that had made you react.

It was a period of great intellectual energy and optimism, even in England where neo-Romantics, led by Dylan Thomas, were on the march and Modernism was still suspected of being a plot by foreigners—Americans, Irishmen, and Europeans—to undermine British culture. For a time during the 1950s, when Beckett's great plays— *Waiting for Godot, Endgame, Krapp's Last Tape*—and poems like Robert Lowell's "The Quaker Graveyard in Nantucket" and Berryman's "Homage to Mistress Bradstreet" first appeared, Modernism and the intellectually demanding standards Eliot had in mind when he talked about Classicism seemed about to prevail, and criticism, moving up a gear to cope with them, became an honorable calling, strenuous and respectable. And because one of the aims of the New Critics was to distinguish between good writing and bad, style mattered to them and they wrote stylishly, thereby raising the standards of literary discourse, even in weekly reviews.

It didn't last, not least because literary matters, both creative and critical, seem to have more in common with the world of fashion than with science. Scientific reputations survive because science develops incrementally, step by step, each advance based on an earlier advance; so in order to understand, say, modern physics, a student must know about Newton and Einstein. Not so in literature, where one set of stylistic rules merely supersedes another. Schools of writing tend to be labeled in decades—the 1930s were political, the '50s conformist, the '60s wild, and so on—and styles of criticism have an even briefer shelf life. According to Frank Kermode, the figures who dominated my student days—I. A. Richards, William Empson, R. P. Blackmur, F. R. Leavis, Northrop Frye, Cleanth Brooks—no longer appear on any student reading lists, and even the great theorist Kenneth Burke wasn't taken up when theory became the fashion.

There is a certain natural justice in this since critics— especially those who have students in their thrall—sometimes get above themselves. The sin of the New Critics was to treat writers as second-class citizens whose function was merely to provide the raw material that the critic then dignified with meaning and relevance. They behaved, that is, as though the critical essay was a work of art equal, if not superior, to the work that provoked it. For this hubris they were duly punished with oblivion. And this is a pity because their occasional delusions of grandeur were founded on a passionate belief that good writing really mattered, not just in itself, but to the lives we lead. Like Matthew

Arnold, they believed that culture had taken over from religion and politics in the battle against anarchy, that the qualities inherent in great literature—sweetness and light, Arnold called them—were in themselves a source of morality, independent of the practitioner, a good you served impartially, as you might dedicate your life to God. In the beginning was the word.

ii

Nowhere was belief in the word stronger than for the writers behind the iron curtain who refused to follow the party line during the four decades before 1989. This in itself was nothing new in Central Europe. In Italo Calvino's novel *If on a Winter's Night a Traveler*, Arkadian Porphyrich, Director General of the State Police Archives of the country of Ircania, has this to say:

> Nobody these days holds the written word in such high esteem as police states do. . . . What statistic allows one to identify the nations where literature enjoys true consideration better than the sums appropriated for controlling it and suppressing it? Where it is the object of such attentions, literature gains an extraordinary authority, inconceivable in countries where it is allowed to vegetate as an innocuous pastime, without risks.[4]

For nearly two centuries, the literature of countries like Poland, Czechoslovakia, and Hungary, which were squeezed between hostile major powers and accustomed to one form or another of foreign domination, had been the object of this dubious style of official attention. In those circumstances, it ceases to be a marginal, leisure-time activity and becomes crypto-politics. One hundred and fifty years ago, for example, the poet Sándor Petőfi was a key figure in Hungarian political life for two equally compelling reasons: because he played a leading role in the 1848 War of Independence and died in battle; and because, in a country where the official language of parliament and law was Latin and the Habsburg court spoke German, he was the first major poet to use the vernacular. According to György Lukács, Petőfi's poem "John the Hero" was doubly important in its day: it was written in the native language, and, for the first time in Hungarian literature, it was also a work in which the Magyar-speaking hero was a peasant with nationalistic ideals, not a nobleman. Together those two elements added up to a revolutionary political act. For the Hungarians, Petőfi is revered both as a major poet and as a national hero. The discussion group where the 1956 anti-Soviet revolution was born was called the Petőfi Club. Similarly, in Poland there is a long and honored tradition of what they call "Aesopian language"— political discussion masquerading as works of the imagination. "All political discussions happened in novels and poems. There were no politics, but there were writers," said Zdzislaw Najder, a literary academic, Conrad scholar, and one-time political exile who eventually returned home to become an adviser to the president of the post-communist Polish government.[5] Borges, who had experienced some of the same pressures, put it even more succinctly: "Censorship is the mother of metaphor."

So when the communist lid came down over Eastern

Europe in 1948, the writers, after their brief democratic honeymoon between the two world wars, found themselves back in a situation they knew depressingly well. The stakes, however, had been raised out of all recognition. Even the most private poets with no political interests at all found themselves politicized willy-nilly, because to write about the private world without reference to the canons of socialist realism was, both by decree and by definition, a subversive activity. They became, that is, what poets in those countries had always been: an opposition in hiding, witnesses for the prosecution. But what was at stake now was not the old game of politics pretending to be poetry, the continuation of politics by other means. It was, instead, something far more important: the survival of ordinary human values—sanity, decency, self-respect—in an ocean of corruption and hypocrisy. The Polish poet Zbigniew Herbert's great poem "The Envoy of Mr Cogito" was more than a refusal to go gently into that good night; it was also a refusal to accept the lies and compromises that made for the good life in communist Poland:

> Go upright among those who are on their knees
> Among those with their backs turned and those toppled in the dust
>
> You were saved not in order to live
> You have little time You must give testimony
>
> Be courageous when the mind deceives you be courageous
> In the final account only this is important

In Poland, Herbert's authority as a poet was moral as well as aesthetic, and that is not a role writers in the West are accustomed to. Milton was probably the last English poet with that degree of ethical prestige, and when Shelley called poets "unacknowledged legislators," he was indulging in the sheerest wishful thinking.

For the dissident writers, an author's integrity could be judged by his tone of voice and his attitude to language. Like George Orwell, they believed "the greatest enemy of clear language is insincerity,"[6] and the language of insincerity is cliché—the debased phrases and dead metaphors that come automatically, without thinking, without any personal input from the writer. Orwell says of empty formulations like these, "If thought corrupts language, language can also corrupt thought." Style, he meant, defines intelligence as well as sensibility; how you write shows how you think.

The Czech novelist Ivan Klíma had another name for cliché; he called it "jerkish." According to Philip Roth, who interviewed Klíma in Prague, in 1990,:

Jerkish is the name of the language developed in the United States some years back for the communication between people and chimpanzees; it consists of 225 words, and Klíma's hero predicts that, after what has happened to his own language under the Communists, it can't be long before jerkish is spoken by all mankind. "Over breakfast," says this writer whom the state will not allow to be published, "I'd read a poem in the paper by the leading author writing in jerkish." The four banal little quatrains are quoted. "For this poem of 69 words," he says," including the title, the author needs a mere 37 jerkish terms and no idea at all. . . . Anyone strong enough to read the poem attentively will realize that for a jerkish poet even a vocabulary of 225 words is needlessly large."[7]

Klíma was talking about the time when Stalinists dictated the cultural rules, and from that bleak perspective "jerkish" was the perfect word—slangy, Americanized, and full of contempt. And because language, behind the iron curtain, was the prime weapon in the struggle against what the Czech poet Miroslav Holub called "codified stupidity," style and morality were inextricably entwined; how you wrote somehow reflected how you behaved as well as how you thought.

"Authenticity," said Holub, "living everyday authenticity, plain human speech, and the most ordinary human situation of these years were not only poetically viable but also the most telling argument . . . [in] the age-old struggle of intellect with codified stupidity."[8] Note that he is not just talking about repression, although repression and censorship were part—maybe the codifying part—of the ambient stupidity. Equally hard to cope with was stupidity in its ordinary sense—the blunted, arrogant, venal crassness of the apparatchiks and the sentimentality of the official style, socialist realism. For Holub, authenticity meant writing poems about everyday life casually and without hysteria because, in a world of agitprop and political self-righteousness, it was private values and private life, even when it was unhappy, that kept people sane, and it was the business of the poet to remind his readers of their shared, troubled humanity.

Similarly, Zbigniew Herbert fought back against the philistinism of the cultural commissars with irony, clarity, and intellectual disdain—in other words, by writing well. His orderly, translucent language made him seem reasonable in a supremely unreasonable time and gave him a moral authority that the Elizabethans or Milton would have called "noble." "Noble" is a word that has long gone out of fashion in the West, but it applies to poets like Herbert and Holub naturally and inevitably, without a hint of pomposity or self-regard. They are noble because in their understated ways they stuck up for what the Ancient Greeks and Romans, whom Herbert loved, called "virtue"—courage, moral discrimination, intellectual probity, and good behavior. And they did so not by moralizing, but by the self-effacing purity of their style.

iii

Herbert thought of himself as a Classicist like Eliot, whose work he revered. But Classicism was a fragile ideal in a country that was, in Sylvia Plath's words, "Scraped flat by the roller / Of wars, wars, wars," and history was not on its side. Throughout the last century every enlightened step forward—in science, technology, social justice, the elimination of poverty and prejudice—was counterbalanced by crazed eruptions of irrationality and barbarism—world wars, genocide, the threat of nuclear holocaust, endemic totalitarianism—symbolized most clearly and brutally by that peculiarly twentieth-century innovation, the death camp, where the technology was used to set up factories for the efficient production of corpses. In the face of such havoc, it became increasingly difficult to believe in the supremacy of order and sweet reason.

The cold war was also a bad time for writers on our side of the iron curtain, though in the Western democracies, where anything goes in the arts and nobody much cares, the sense of strain was harder to locate. American novelists like Joan Didion, Robert Stone and Don DeLillo, who came into their own in the late 1960s and '70s, responded to the general unease with a subliminal but endemic paranoia. Didion's word for it is "dread," by which she meant an intense disquiet that invades and subverts every detail of the otherwise hedonistic and well-heeled world around her. For Stone, the paranoia is rawer, more immediate, more urgent, and seemingly more drug related; everything in his novels reeks of threat and everybody is part of some obscure plot his helpless but sardonic heroes don't quite understand. DeLillo has a more sidelong take on the ambient dread—detached, witty, experimental, fragmented, seemingly even a little schizoid—a vision of disaster illuminated by strobe lights. What they share is the conviction that there is something badly wrong with the system and they are stuck with it.

Thirty years ago, in a book called *The Savage God*, I tried to suggest what that something might be and how the artists evolved a style to cope with it. I called it Extremism, by which I meant an art that goes out along that friable edge between the tolerable and intolerable, yet does so with all the discipline and clarity and attention to detail Eliot implied when he talked of Classicism. Where the Extremist poets—Robert Lowell, John Berryman, Sylvia Plath, above all—parted company with Eliot was not in his devotion to the stern discipline of art, but in his belief in what he called "the continual extinction of personality." Extremist artists, the Abstract Expressionist painters as well as the poets, deliberately used their chaotic personal lives—Lowell was manic-depressive, Berryman and Jackson Pollock were alcoholics, Plath and Rothko were depressed to the point of borderline psychosis—to set up a mirror to the chaos out there in the world. "To extreme sicknesses, extreme remedies," wrote Montaigne, but even at their most extreme they never betrayed their Modernist belief in art as a serious business that doesn't come easily and is, by its very nature, difficult and challenging.

This high-minded devotion to high culture has not just grown remote and outdated in the last couple of decades, it has also come to seem morally suspect. It is as though the spirit of Stalin had risen again, fifty years after his death and despite the collapse of communism. Jerkish and the codified stupidity that went with it continue to flourish, though now they have been made over, as it were, by Hollywood: the sentimentality and unearned rectitude of socialist realism have been replaced by the equally sentimental and intolerant moral coercion of political correctness, and the power of kitsch and cliché remains irresistible. The cliché for this process is "dumbing-down."

Socialist realism and political correctness are united in

their distrust of highbrow art, especially the demanding
and essentially private art of poetry. The Marxists called it
"bourgeois and decadent"; nowadays the dismissive epithet
is "elitist." For someone of my generation, this seems peculiarly ironic. Half a century ago, when poetry was difficult
and judgment mattered, belonging to an intellectual elite
had nothing to do with politics or privilege and everything to do with how you used your education. It was
simply what happened when you studied a subject in
detail, thought about it, and reached your own conclu-
sions. Edmund Wilson, who had no truck with the New
Criticism or the universities, put it this way:

> How, you may ask, can we identify this elite who know
> what they are talking about? Well, it can only be said of
> them that they are self-appointed and self-perpetuating,
> and that they will compel you to accept their authority.
> Impostors may try to put themselves over, but these
> quacks will not last. The implied position of the people
> who know about literature (as is also the case in every
> other art) is simply that they know what they know.[9]

Wilson was supremely a man who knew what he knew,
and one of the things he knew was that his audience
shared his assumptions. This was the same audience that
the editors of *Partisan Review* relied on when they wrote,
in 1953:

> As we see him, this ideal reader is receptive to new
> work in fiction, poetry, and art, is aware of the major
> tendencies in contemporary criticism, is concerned with

the structure and fate of modern society, in particular
with the precise nature and menace of Communism, is
informed or wishes to become informed about new
currents in psychoanalysis and the other humanistic
sciences, is opposed to such "nativist" demagogues as
Senator McCarthy and to all other varieties of know-
nothingism, and feels above all that what happens in
literature and the arts has a direct effect on the quality
of his own life.[10]

That style of educated and intellectually curious audience
still exists, but I think it is becoming steadily more belea-
guered. So where did it all go wrong?

iv

We tend to think that the rift between creative writers and
intellectuals opened up late in the '60s, when drugs became
the common cause that separated the young from the old.
This is not strictly true. The Beatniks may have helped
create the drug culture that climaxed during the later
stages of the Vietnam War, but the Beat generation itself
took off in the previous decade, during the placid, prosper-
ous years of Eisenhower's presidency, when the New Criticism was at its height and the domestic issue that provoked
greatest anxiety among intellectuals was smugness and conformism. "We are a nation of 20 million bathtubs," Mary
McCarthy wrote disdainfully, "with a humanist in every
tub."[11] The Beat writers were also bothered by conformism,
but for them conformism meant Modernism and the New

Critics who served it. So, under the baton of Allen Ginsberg, they rebelled against it in the name of spontaneity and spirituality, though their motives, I think, were more political than aesthetic.

Ginsberg brought two things to the literary party in the 1950s and they went together: he wrote in the manner of Walt Whitman and he had passion for William Blake. Ginsberg's Blake, however, was not the poet who wrote the taut, dislocating *Songs of Innocence and Experience*; he was the dotty, long-winded Blake of the Prophetic Books, free-associating his own mythology as he went along. This rambling, often ranting style was an excuse for the rambling and usually drug-induced formlessness of the Beats. For them, dope was a shortcut to bardic inspiration and it went with their belief in the wisdom of madness, as preached at the time by R. D. Laing.

Nobody quite knows where the Beats got their name: was it short for beatific or did it just mean exhausted? All that is certain is that they were determined to shock the intelligentsia as well as the bourgeoisie, and they resented everything that the New Critics and the great Modernists stood for. That, I think, is one reason why Ginsberg chose to write like Whitman, a poet who was much out of favor at the time because he used free verse to talk at the top of his voice rather than to follow, T. E. Hulme–style, the movement of his sensibility. Ginsberg's other reason was equally polemical. Philip Rahv had written a famous essay about the two opposing groups of American writers, "Paleface and Redskin" he called them, the aesthetes and the wild men, Boston and the frontier, patrician and plebeian, "the drawing-room fictions of Henry James and the open air poems of Walt Whitman."[12] So to write in the bardic style of Whitman or of Blake's Prophetic Books at a time when most other poets were struggling with the inheritance of John Donne and T. S. Eliot was a gesture of defiance.

As gestures went though, it was too restricted, too literary, too academic for the Beats. Someone once said that New York in the 1930s was the most interesting part of the Soviet Union because it was only there that debates between Stalinists and Trotskyites could be conducted openly, without show trials or executions. Twenty years later, the debates were still going on, but they had changed the terms from politics to literature and they called it the New Criticism. Ginsberg had been brought up among Bohemian Marxists—his father was a failed poet and a socialist, his schizophrenic mother was a Stalinist—and he called himself "a political [poet] or a visionary activist."[13] In 1958, when the Beat generation was first grabbing the headlines, Norman Mailer shrewdly remarked, "The beatnik—often Jewish—comes from the middle-class, and 25 years ago would have joined the YCL."[14] Since the Young Communist League was no longer an option and, with Joe McCarthy on the prowl, capitalism was a touchy subject, the next best target was highbrow art, and the equivalent of radical politics was dope.

"Howl" famously begins, "I saw the best minds of my generation destroyed by madness, starving hysterical naked, / dragging themselves through the negro streets at dawn looking for an angry fix. . . ." "The best minds of his generation?" someone remarked to me at the time. "It makes you wonder whom he met." In fact, Ginsberg had studied at Columbia under Lionel Trilling, so he must have known plenty of clever people, but they weren't the ones who interested him. He preferred "angelheaded hipsters burning for the ancient heavenly connection to the starry dynamo in the machinery of night." In other words, he reinvented the addicts and misfits who were his friends as a new proletariat, a spiritual proletariat with a taste for Eastern mysticism. "Dreamers of the world unite. You have nothing to lose but your karma."

It is impossible to overestimate the anti-intellectualism of the Beat generation. They were know-nothings in revolt against the know-alls, and in their war against their highbrow enemies dope was the perfect weapon. They regarded it as a way of cutting through inhibitions at a peculiarly inhibited time, but I suspect this mattered less than distancing themselves from square society. Because drugs were "controlled substances," when those angelheaded hipsters turned on, tuned in, and dropped out, they were putting themselves outside the law. More important, drugs don't agree with the intellectual life. To the impartial observer outside the stoned circle, the most obvious feature of cannabis and LSD is that they constrict thought more than they expand the mind. Dope may make you feel good but it doesn't do much for the conversation. John Berryman, a chronic alcoholic but a fierce intellect, wrote in one of his guilt-drenched "Dream Songs," "This is not for tears; / thinking." But you can't think when you're stoned. You can't, in fact, register anything much

except vague goodwill. When Joan Didion wrote her wonderful report on the hippies of San Francisco, "Slouching
Towards Bethlehem," what came across most strongly was
her dismay at the mindlessness of Beatnik existence as it
was played out on the streets of San Francisco.

She was witnessing, I think, a mid-twentieth-century
rerun of the Romantic agony in its prime. The essence of
Romantic genius is revelation and the exultation and certainty that go with it. (Think of Wordsworth at Tintern
Abbey, Keats and the Grecian urn, or even "stout Cortez"
gazing out over the Pacific with "a wild surmise.") But
revelation can't be willed or worked for; it is more like a
blessing, something that might happen to you if you live
right. Hence, Coleridge's curiously passive image—in
"Dejection: an Ode"—of the poet as an Aeolian harp
blown upon by forces beyond his control. This is inspiration in the most literal sense, and if it can't be deliberately
ordered up, it can at least be provoked and encouraged.
Hence, the Romantics' preoccupation with dreams, or
rather, with nightmares. All young Romantics, good and
bad, gifted and foolish, were besotted with what Shelley
called "the tempestuous loveliness of terror." "The sleep of
reason breeds monsters" said Goya, and the Romantics
went to great lengths to waken those monsters. The
painter Fuseli, for example, guzzled platefuls of raw meat
and rotting food late at night in order to provoke nightmares; so did Ann Radcliffe, who wrote *The Mysteries of
Udolpho*, one of the most famous of all Gothick novels; so
did many other lesser figures. The artists gave themselves
bad dreams and indigestion in the name of inspiration in

the same hopeful, masochistic spirit as the young women of the time tortured themselves in the name of High Romance: they drank vinegar and sucked lead pencils to make their faces pale and melancholy, dilated their pupils with belladonna for luminous eyes, starved themselves and wore iron corsets for a sylphlike figure—all because they wanted to look like the heroines of the Gothick novels they devoured, while young men strutted around in blue tailcoats and yellow waistcoats, threatening suicide, like their hero Werther. The lost children of Haight-Ashbury were much the same: they hankered after spiritual drama and significance, but, because they lacked the talent, patience, and application that art requires, they had to make do with drugs and fancy dress.

This sensationalist aspect of nineteenth-century Romanticism, which had more to do with fashion than creativity, was a sad parody of the serious artists' belief that dreaming and poetic creation were parallel and interchangeable worlds, intimately linked. Although the word 'unconscious' had not yet entered the language in its modern sense, Romantic poets believed that a hotline to their dream life was a necessary part of their professional equipment.

The Romantics also took opium, though not, initially, as a source of inspiration. According to Althea Hayter, the use of opium as a painkiller and soporific is literally as old as the practice of medicine: "In an Egyptian medical treatise of the sixteenth century BC, Theban physicians were advised to prescribe opium for crying children just as, three and a half millennia later, Victorian babies were dosed with the opiate Godfrey's Cordial by their nurses to keep them quiet."[15] Until late in the nineteenth century, opium was generally available as a cure for everything. It was like aspirin; every household had some, usually in the form of laudanum—that is, mixed with alcohol—and used it as an analgesic for aches and pains, for hangovers, toothache, and hysteria. Shelley drank laudanum to calm his nervous headaches, Keats used it as a painkiller, Byron took an opium-based concoction called Kendal Black Drop as a tranquilizer, and Jane Austen's sedate mother prescribed it for travel sickness. It was also classless and cheap, so cheap that factory workers in the earliest "dark satanic mills" swilled laudanum on Saturday nights because it cost less than booze, even at a time when you could get "drunk for a penny, dead drunk for tuppence." When Marx called religion "the opium of the masses," the masses would have known what he meant.

Naturally, the general availability of opium and the medical profession's enthusiasm for it helped create addicts, some of them very famous: Clive of India, for example, and William Wilberforce, the great emancipator. Among the literary addicts, Coleridge and Thomas De Quincy were the best known, but they also included that most sober poet George Crabbe. (Oddly enough, William Blake, the hippies' hero, was not an opium eater; but then, he was so eccentric that he started where opium left off.) All of them, however, were addicts despite themselves, not by design but by mistake, by misfortune, by chance. At a time when doctors themselves had no concept of addiction, there was nothing to alert their patients to the dangers of the patent medicines they prescribed or to prepare them for the side effects. As a result, there was no more stigma attached to the opium habit than to alcoholism; it was an unfortunate weakness, not a vice.

And for the poets, the effects of the drug were sometimes astonishing, at least in the early stages of addiction. Witness Coleridge's famous description of the genesis of "Kubla Khan":

> In consequence of a slight indisposition, an anodyne had been prescribed, from the effects of which he fell asleep in his chair at the moment when he was reading the following sentence . . . in "Purchas's Pilgrimage": "Here the Kubla Khan commanded a palace to be built, and a stately garden thereunto. And thus ten miles of fertile ground were enclosed with a wall." The Author continued for about three hours in a profound sleep, at least of the external senses, during which time he has the most vivid confidence, that he could not have composed less than from two to three hundred lines; if that indeed could be called composition in which all the images rose up before him as *things*, with a parallel production of the correspondent expression, without any sensation or consciousness of effort. On awakening he appeared to have a distinct recollection of the whole, and taking his pen, ink, and paper, instantly and eagerly wrote down the lines that are here preserved.[16]

This is at once a paradigm of Romantic inspiration—the poet as Aeolian harp—and also, incidentally, a most seductive come-on for the use of drugs as a shortcut to creativity.

"Kubla Khan" may have been a one-off phenomenon,

but Coleridge learned from it and it had a profound effect on the two great poems that followed. "The Rime of the Ancient Mariner" and "Christabel" are steeped in hallucination and dreams: nightmare shifts of focus like the swift, secret, chilling transformation of the face of "the lovely lady Geraldine" into a serpent's, or of the ocean into a putrid pond; also hallucinatory distortions of time and place, such as the Mariner's eternity becalmed, then his seemingly overnight flit from the Pacific to England. Coleridge had always been a wonderfully subtle observer and interpreter of his own states of mind—both a psychoanalyst and an analysand *avant la lettre*—and part of his genius was his ability to tap into his underlife—his hallucinations, dreams, and anxieties as well as his prodigious learning—not just for images but as a source of poetry, as a way of re-creating the strangeness of the inner world. He used his experiences under opium to fuse together what he called the *ego diurnus* and the *ego nocturnus*, the day-self and the night-self. The result was a genuinely altered state of aesthetic consciousness, a precursor of the systematic deregulation of the senses that Rimbaud talked about later.

Yet even Coleridge could not make it last. The three great poems were written during the relatively blissful honeymoon period when opium was still a source of inspiration, an enabler of his imagination. The dreams that came later, when he was seriously addicted, were altogether more threatening and unforgiving, like those described by De Quincy in *Confessions of an English Opium-Eater*. The habit had killed what Coleridge called his "shaping spirit of imagination"—his emotional energy, his delight in poetry, his appetite for life. He wrote one great poem, "Dejection," about the inner desolation that drug addiction creates, then, despite reams of indifferent verse, he turned mostly to prose. But he knew precisely what he had lost. In 1815, with all his great poems long behind him, he wrote in his notebook, "If a man could pass thro' Paradise in a Dream & have a flower presented to him as a pledge that his Soul had really been there, and found that flower in his hand when he awoke—Aye! and what then?" I think the paradise he was talking about was the period of seemingly effortless opium-fueled inspiration and the masterpieces he produced in his youthful prime. And the flower in his hand was a poppy.

v

Coleridge may have ended up as an addict, but only by accident and he wasn't initially interested in opium in or for itself. Like any writer, of course, he was enraptured by the idea of blissful, effortless inspiration, but he was interested even more in the states of mind drugs produced— insights, images, hallucinations, and all the other strange mental disjunctions that were part of the mystery of the self that the Romantics, at the end of the classical eighteenth century, were suddenly free to explore.

In the age of Freud, 150 years later, the self had lost its mysteries and the Beatniks were writing for young audiences that believed it was their democratic duty, as well as their right, to display and sometimes act out their psychopathology in public. And because the politics of drug taking seemed to have mattered to the Beats more than the drugs themselves, their altered states of consciousness had no aesthetic consequences. Ginsberg wrote several poems with titles like "Mescaline," "Lysergic Acid," and "A Methedrine Vision in Hollywood," but there is nothing in them to suggest that the drugs altered his style one jot. The roll-call of images may be more wilfully loopy than usual and the connections between them more haphazard—though not by much—but the exclamatory, chanting, curiously monotonous tone of voice is no different from his poems about landscapes or presidential conventions.

This is the paradox of Beat writing. When it first appeared—or rather, after the publication of Ginsberg's lament for his dead mother, "Kaddish"—it was labeled "Confessional" because it seemed to be talking about the kind of intimate material that is usually whispered only to a priest or a psychotherapist. Yet it did so in a public and rather boastful voice, the voice of the *ego diurnus* pronouncing on the *ego nocturnus,* and the subsequent effect on the arts has been profound.

In 1966, I attended a reading Ginsberg gave at New York State University in Buffalo. The audience was too large for a lecture hall, so he gave it in the basketball arena, which had banked seating for hundreds. But the PA system wasn't working, so you couldn't hear him, and the clouds of pot smoke were so thick you could scarcely see him. Even so, the kids were having a wonderful time. He tinkled his bells and chanted his poems and the audience responded with a kind of collective "Wow!" It wasn't about communication, it was about communion—everyone joined by a sense of vague well-being, more like a religious ceremony or a political rally than a poetry reading. And that suited the verse just fine. There's no way you can read a Ginsberg poem on the page and get much aesthetic pleasure from it. It has to be declaimed, performed. Poetry of this kind is not a private experience, it's a public phenomenon, a happening, and—most important of all—anyone can do it. And that, I think, was the secret of the Beat writers' appeal: they made the audiences feel that they, too, were bards like them, initiates of the same hip clan. You didn't even have to be mad, Ronnie Laing–style—shut away in the back ward of an institution or wandering the streets, muttering to yourself, with everything you owned piled into a supermarket cart. All that was required was to be there at the love-in, mellowed out on weed or tripping on LSD, and you, too, could be a poet, no matter whether or not you ever got words down on the page.

I now understand that what I was witnessing that evening in Buffalo was something new and strange: the transformation of poetry into showbiz. Back then, poets sometimes recorded their work, though mainly for university archives, but public readings were rare and mostly confined to the Soviet Union, where the verse on offer—the stars were Yevgeny Yevtushenko and Andrei Voznesensky—was less interesting to literary people than to Kremlinologists, who studied it not as art but as a measure of Premier Khrushchev's thaw. In America, I think Robert Frost was the only established poet to read regularly to large audiences. Even Yeats, who dressed the part of the romantic poet and had a flair for drama, rarely performed in public.

Poets were private people and reading their work was still a private pleasure.

Ginsberg changed all that by sheer force of personality. Or rather, by using verse as a vehicle for showmanship, he helped turn a minority art into a form of popular entertainment based on the cult of personality. Whence the busy contemporary reading circuit, with its bards and buskers, its wild men, wild women, and professional charmers, and an audience for whom the language of the poems matters less than the panache of the performers and the frankness with which they reveal their souls. It was as though all Jean Rhys's worst nightmares had come true: instead of using their art to redeem the mess they had made of their lives, the Beats served the mess up uncooked and called it poetry.

F. R. Leavis once dismissed the Sitwells because, he said, they belonged more to the history of advertising than to the history of poetry. True enough, but the Sitwells, being vainglorious and snobbish, at least presented themselves as being immeasurably avant garde. Similarly, Ezra Pound was a showman, a consummate promoter of new styles and new writers, but his passion was for the art of poetry and he used his promotional skills to educate his audience, to open their ears to fresh ideas and unexpected ways of speaking, and thereby raise the standard of literary discourse. That, presumably, was what he meant when he said that poetry should be at least as well written as prose. Not so the Beats. They were a populist movement that was blessed by having as their ringmaster a publicist—and self-publicist—of genius.

The Beat writers at their best were laid back and good humored, but they were not as harmless as they first seemed, and they set a benchmark for what was to follow. Quite simply, they meant what they said when they talked about the "counterculture": they were truly counter—that is, against—culture, and their reasons for being so were political. Inherent in their attitude to drugs as a source of inspiration democratically available to everyone, regardless of talent as well as race, color, creed, and education, is a process of artistic and intellectual downgrading not far removed from the philistinism of the Soviet cultural commissars. Andrei Zhdanov, Stalin's artistic dictator and censor-in-chief, would have approved, so would Ginsberg's Stalinist mother, and Holub would have recognized the symptoms from his student days in Prague, after the communist coup in 1948:

> The leader of the communist students announced that the [Students'] Union had just been dissolved and a blind hysterical sort of *yurodivy* ["visionary"], young man began screaming about his vision of the May Day parade in which we would all march and sing the Russian songs.
>
> At that moment I realized that there is no poetry not only because of Auschwitz, that there are no words, that there is no identity, that we are completely isolated in the crowds of quasi-*yurodivy* colleagues, that there is no "civilian" poetry. . . . And no programme except to shut up.[17]

The dissident writers, of course, didn't shut up. Instead, they wrote, as they used to say, "for the desk drawer," knowing their work might never be published. But that was a disappointment that did not concern them and it affected their tone not one jot. Their poems are ironic, even-handed, intransigent, without what Zbigniew Herbert called "false warmth," yet shot through with feeling. It was enough that their "civilian" poetry should be perfect in its own terms and for its own sake, with or without an audience.

Although the Beat writers have become just another footnote in literary history, we are now living with the aesthetic consequences of their antics: socialist realism transformed by free enterprise into free-market Surrealism. The result is poetry as feel-good entertainment and, above all, the belief that any old confession or self-revelation is intrinsically artistic because an artist is not someone who uses skill and insight to create a work of art with a life of its own; instead, he is a public personality, a performer whose primary work of art is himself and whose ambition is to make himself known.

This shift from art to marketing was not confined to writers. The visual art world's answer to Ginsberg was Andy Warhol, who started out as a window dresser for Saks Fifth Avenue and finished with an art factory that turned out lithographs and silk screens of images he chose—most of them of people even more famous than himself—which he then authenticated with his signature. Warhol was also responsible for defining the purpose of it all: fifteen minutes of fame, an idea that culminates in a figure like Brit Art's Tracey Emin, who aspires to the condition of pop star and has made a cult of herself instead of her work. Emin's life in the shape of her unmade bed, complete with surrounding detritus, is enshrined in the museum of Charles Saatchi, king of British advertising, and more people know about her sad early years—all booze and bad sex and abortions—than have seen even reproductions of her works.

vi

It is ironic that the cult of personality should have flour-ished in a century that began, after all, with Freud's *Interpretation of Dreams*, a book that seems now like a blueprint for Modernism. Or rather, because experiment in the arts always involves an element of inner or psychic explo-ration, it seems like a rough guide for the inward journey the Modernists took: they wanted to make it new, not for the sake of novelty but because the style at hand wasn't adequate to what they had to express. Some of the Mod-ernists took drugs and most of them drank too much, but they never pretended dope and booze were indispensable to their experiments, nor did they use them as excuses for shoddy work. Similarly, when writers like Lowell turned to their private lives as a source of inspiration, they may have gone against Eliot's strictures on the necessary impersonality of art, but they never betrayed him aestheti-cally or intellectually. That is why it is wrong to lump them together with the Beats as Confessional poets. Berryman's "This is not for tears; thinking" is an altogether sterner recipe for creativity than the free-associating Confessional style that Ginsberg called his "new method of Poetry. All you got to do is lay [sic] down on a couch and think of anything that comes into your head."[18] In other words, let it all hang out any old way, then lie back and bask in the applause—which is not quite how Freud imagined the talking cure should proceed.

High principles and aesthetic conscience notwithstanding, the Extremists, too, eventually succumbed to the confusion between art and life, but they did so in an edgier, more dangerous way that Freud might have understood. They set out deliberately to confront their demons in the cellars of the unconscious and made art out of the mayhem that followed. It was a heroic enterprise, like Theseus slaying the Minotaur, but out of it emerged what I call the myth of the artist, and it is not what I had in mind when I wrote about Extremist art and suicide in *The Savage God*.

Initially, the myth was based on the terrible precedent set by Sylvia Plath, and the tragic way in which her life and her art complete each other. Elizabeth Hardwick, who admires Plath's writing and is appalled by her story, has this to say: "She, the poet, is frighteningly there all the time. Orestes rages but Aeschylus lives to be almost seventy. Sylvia Plath, however, is both heroine and author; when the curtain goes down, it is her own dead body there on the stage, sacrificed to her plot."[19] Plath, of course, was by no means the first important artist to die dramatically by her own hand. Almost two hundred years before her, Thomas Chatterton committed suicide and became, as a result, a great Romantic symbol. But at least he didn't write about the act. Neither did Hemingway or Hart Crane or Randall Jarrell or even, in so many words, Virginia Woolf. To follow the logic of your art to its desolate end, as Sylvia Plath did, and thereby turn yourself into the heroine of a myth that you yourself have created was something unprecedented. It changed the nature of the game. Art, that most stringent and solitary of disciplines, suddenly came to resemble a high-risk activity, like skydiving.

If nothing else, it was one in the eye for the Freudian theory of art as compensation and self-therapy, as D. H. Lawrence described it: "One sheds one's sicknesses in books—repeats and presents one's emotions to be master of them." I myself believe that this is the exact opposite of the truth: you don't shed your sicknesses, you dredge them up in writing and thereby make them readily available to you, so that you find yourself living them out. Nature, that is, always imitates art, usually in a sloppy and exaggerated way.

John Berryman, for instance, began his great cycle of Dream Songs as a kind of poetic daybook, recording his gripes, hangovers, alcoholic guilts, and very occasional highs. Then he gradually deepened it into an extended act of mourning for various friends tragically dead before their time. That, in turn, led back to what was, for him, the primal suicide—that of his father, who shot himself when Berryman was twelve. And so on, back and back, deeper and deeper, until in the end—particularly in the beautiful series of Dream Songs entitled "Opus Posthumous"—he seemed to be writing his own epitaph, as if there were no one else he could trust with the job. At which point, the way was clear to take his own life. Which he did. It seemed—perversity notwithstanding—the most logical means of completing his magnum opus.

That, anyway, is how the public seemed to read the story of Berryman's desperate and messy last years: portrait of the artist painting himself into a corner. Portrait also of a situation that has got out of hand, for it is based on a total misunderstanding of the nature of art. It is utterly untrue to believe that Extremist art, or any other art, has to be vindicated or justified by an Extremist life, or that the artist's experience on the outer edge of the intolerable is in any way a substitute for creativity. In fact, the opposite is true, as I have written elsewhere again and again: in order to make art out of deprivation and despair the artist needs proportionately rich internal resources and proportionately strict control of his medium. We have the collected works of Samuel Beckett to prove the point. An artist is what he is not because he has lived a more dramatic life than other people, but because his inner world is richer and more available and also, more importantly, because he loves and understands whichever medium he uses— language, paint, music, film, stone—and wants to explore its possibilities and make of it something perfect. I think it was Camus who once remarked that Nietzsche's work proves that you can live a life of wildest adventure without ever leaving your desk. With all due deference to the late Ronnie Laing, schizophrenia is not necessarily a state of grace and there are no shortcuts to creative ability, not even through the psychiatric wards of the most progressive mental hospitals.

But schizophrenia, alas, is a good deal more common than creative ability, so it is not hard to understand why Laing's theories should have been so appealing, especially to the bards of the drug culture. What is baffling is that more disciplined and reticent poets should have gone along so readily with them. How else, for instance, to explain the astonishing lack of professionalism in Anne Sexton's books? Her trouble was not that she wrote bad poems, as every poet does from time to time, but that, instead of throwing them away, she printed them cheek-by-jowl with her purest work. The reason was, I suspect, that the bad poems were bad in much the same way as the good were good: in their head-on intimacy and their persistence in exploring whatever was most painful to her. She was unable to resist the temptation to draw attention to the raw material, as though whatever was sufficiently naked and overwhelming just couldn't fail. As Randall Jarrell once wrote in an essay about amateur verse, "It is as if the writers had sent you their ripped-out arms and legs, with 'This is a poem' scrawled on them in lipstick."[20]

The truth is, great tragic poems are not necessarily inspired by great tragedies. On the contrary, they can be precipitated, like pearls, by the smallest irritants, provided the poet's secret, internal world is rich enough. William Empson once remarked that the opening line of Keats's "Ode to Melancholy"—"No, no; go not to Lethe; neither twist . . ."—"tells you that somebody, or some force in the poet's mind, must have wanted to go to Lethe very much, if it took four negatives in the first line to stop them."[21] By the same token, the more exposed and painful the theme, the more delicate and alert the artistic control needed to handle it. According to a psychoanalyst, Hanna Segal,[22] there is a fundamental difference between the neurotic and the artist: the neurotic is at the mercy of his neurosis, whereas the artist, however neurotic he may be outside his work, has *in his capacity as an artist* a highly realistic understanding both of his inner world and of the techniques of his art.

For example, Anne Sexton's good poems have an expressive tautness and inevitability in the rhythm that not only drive them forward but also keep them whole. In her bad poems, the need to express gives way to an altogether less trustworthy inspiration—the sheer pleasure of confessing, of letting it all hang out in public—and you can hear it in the way the rhythm slackens and blurs into hypnotic chanting. What begin as real poems end in an operatic no-man's-land, the shadow zone between Grand Opera and soap opera.

That in itself is nothing new. All sorts of talented writers have had their moments on the borderline of hysteria— Shelley, for instance, Dostoyevsky, Lawrence. To lose one's poise is an occupational hazard for an original artist, exploring the unknown. The specifically modern ingredient Anne Sexton and lesser poets added to the mixture was not that they occasionally lost control and thus became hysterical, but that they were hysterical *on purpose*. The poetry, that is, not only became indistinguishable from the psychopathology, it became secondary to it.

In the same way, the myth of the artist and the cult of personality became indistinguishable when they were taken up by the media. Art fashions may be news of a kind, but the scandalous lives of artists make much better news. "Real art," Susan Sontag said, "has the capacity to make us nervous." Not so real artists, who tend to be battered, fallible, and tiresomely self-centered. So by concentrating on them and their unspeakable lives, you conveniently sidestep the effects of their art. I wonder to what extent Dylan Thomas's so-called friends and admiring, ox-eyed public secretly envied him his genius and therefore encouraged him to drink himself to death in the name of good companionship and the Romantic idea of what a Bohemian poet's life should be. It is much the same with Sylvia Plath: everyone knows about her broken marriage and despair and suicide, but how many of the thousands who have gobbled up her intensely autobiographical novel, *The Bell Jar,* have ever bothered with her sardonic, unforgiving, yet curiously detached poems? Similarly, her husband Ted Hughes's *Birthday Letters* probably became a best-seller not because of the beauty and power of his lan-guage, but because people wanted the lowdown on his marriage to Plath.

Writing, however, is a solitary pursuit, as monotonous as psychoanalysis, though more lonely because you don't even get to see patients. So it is easy, in your lighthouse keeper's isolation, to be taken in by your own propaganda and begin to believe the myth you yourself have created. Moreover, fame is addictive, particularly if you practise a nonpaying, minority art like poetry, and even a poet as devoted, intellectually resolute, and lavishly gifted as John Berryman was unable to resist it. He and Lowell had made it aesthetically respectable to use their private lives as a source for their poems, but they did so while still believing in the essential impersonality of art, as Eliot described it: "Poetry is not the turning loose of emotion, but an escape from emotion; it is not the expression of personality, but an escape from personality. But, of course, only those who have personality and emotions know what it means to want to escape from these things."[23] Plath believed that, too, until the personality and emotions she tapped into turned out to be beyond her control. Her terrible death and subsequent fame created a cruel aftershock in the poets she outlived and changed their attitude to their art.

Berryman once remarked, in a *Paris Review* interview, "The artist is extremely lucky who is presented with the worst possible ordeal which will not actually kill him. At that point, he's in business."[24] This sounds like the old Romantic Agony buttressed by mid-twentieth-century theories: a theory of existentialist aesthetics and a simplified psychoanalytic theory of the therapeutic relationship of art to life. If you think about this kind of statement, then remember how Berryman died, how Sylvia Plath died, how Anne Sexton died—all of them passionately believing that this was how the game was played—you have to conclude that no poetry, however fine, is worth the cost.

But there was another element involved, less tragic, less heroic: Berryman's remark, that is, was also influenced by his intense, competitive involvement with the media and with the idea of fame. Not long before he died, Berryman wrote an indifferent autobiographical novel, *Recovery*, with a polymath hero who seems to embody all the author's most grandiose fantasies: he is Alan Severance, M.D., Litt.D., a professor of immunology and molecular biology who also teaches a humanities course on the side. Like Berryman, Dr. Severance is an alcoholic who is being dried out. Like Berryman, too, he has been interviewed by both *Time* and *Life* and can't get over it. Berryman has this to say of him: "Severance was a conscientious man. He had really thought, off and on for twenty years, that it was his duty to drink, namely, to sacrifice himself. He saw the products as worth it."[25] As a rationale for alcoholism, this strikes me as being as fanciful and self-aggrandizing as Severance himself. It becomes convincing only when you turn it inside out: given Berryman's belief in the connection between art and agony, given also the public's appetite for bad behavior in its artists (which deflects it from the necessity of taking their work seriously), it may be that, for Berryman, writing poetry was an excuse for his drinking.

At that point art itself becomes a sideshow of no genuine intrinsic value. All that matters is the disturbance from which art might emerge, given the right, distraught talent and the right, disastrous circumstances. In other words, the artists whom the '60s public found most alluring were those who knowingly cooperated in their own destruction. Having created myths of themselves as a by-product of creating art, they finished by sacrificing themselves to those essentially trivial myths.

Maybe this desperation was a reaction to something in the political air: the cold war, nuclear threat, Vietnam. Extremism was the last gasp of the Modernist movement, experimentation taken to its logical, in-turning conclusion, and it could only have happened in a period of high anxiety. The stakes now are smaller and poetry is milder, less adventurous. I wouldn't want all that trouble back, but the work that came out of it was great while it lasted.

vii

I wonder if Extremism wasn't also the last gasp of the traditional belief in art that is disciplined, difficult, and unembarrassed by the fact that it is not politically correct. "To write on their plan," as Dr. Johnson said, "it was at least necessary to read and think." It was also necessary to make judgments about what was good art and what was not, and those are concepts no longer encouraged by the institutions designed to protect them. I wonder, in short, if the conflation of the arts and showbiz hasn't been reinforced, by the way literature is now studied at universities.

To put it simply, the general public seems more interested in the personalities of live authors and the biographies of dead ones because, among other reasons, it is no longer taught to read. Paradoxically, it may be the New Critics who are to blame. They believed that by teaching students to read closely, the study of literature would be changed from a soft option into something tougher and more demanding. But to read in that style was, as I said, an art in itself; it implied a feeling for language and a degree of insight into the way the minds of writers work, and those are not necessarily qualifications that count for much in universities. Modern English departments have become intellectually strenuous in ways the New Critics could never have imagined, but only at the expense of literature itself. Creative writing, especially as it is embodied in what they call "the canon," has come to seem a trivial pursuit, only peripherally relevant to the business of academic criticism. Texts matter less than their contexts, and the earnest insistence on theory, politics, race, gender, and whatever else goes to make up the paranoia about "dead white males" has eliminated the idea of major and minor writers. By doing so, it has also built an iron curtain between academic criticism and the art of writing. When literature is studied primarily from an extraliterary and politically correct point of view, value judgments become a form of cultural imperialism and you avoid them because you are afraid of appearing elitist.

How this terror of elitism manages to reconcile itself with the impenetrable, jargon-filled prose in which it is expressed is hard to understand, but the outcome is clear enough: by abjuring value judgments and concentrating on theoretical and political issues, university teachers have turned literature into just another arcane and self-referential academic discipline. This discipline may have a satisfying coherence and even a formal elegance all its own, but it has nothing to do with imaginative writing. If you can't or won't explain why you think, say, one poem is better than another or how this novel works and that one doesn't, then you are setting yourself apart from the business of writing as the writer sees it—apart, that is, from the continual process of self-criticism and self-doubt, and the whole sorry drudgery that goes into creating an authentic voice, without which there can be no work of art. And that, too, is another idea that is in danger of being lost: the concept of the work of art as something perfect, a supreme fiction that can be ruined by a single word out of place.

Perfection of this kind makes even a lyric as brief as Yeats's "Memory" seem as indestructible as stone, its structure held together by both inner and outer tension—by the pared-down expression of feeling and absolute economy of form:

> *One had a lovely face,*
> *And two or three had charm,*
> *But charm and face were in vain*
> *Because the mountain grass*
> *Cannot but keep the form*
> *Where the mountain hare has lain.*

Consider the casual tone of the opening, the throwaway half-rhymes—face/grass, charm/form—then the sudden shift of key in that extraordinary final image. Once you have known perfection, Yeats is saying, everything else is diminished; the mark made by that most elusive creature, the mountain hare, never fades. And he does so in six lines, thirty-three words, and a single, brilliant metaphor, without ever raising his voice. The poem is both about perfection and in itself perfect. It is also a perfect illustration of what Pascal meant when he said, "True eloquence mocks eloquence."

True eloquence is harder than it looks. You take language—this common stuff we use all the time—and you make it precise and personal. Not precise in the finicky way of lawyers or civil servants, who are usually wasteful with words and long-winded, or personal in a loose-lipped confessional way; still less by shoving together ready-made lumps of language—clichés—which is how it is done by politicians and pundits and all those people whose gift, said Karl Kraus, is "to know nothing and to be able to express it." I mean, instead, expressing precisely what you have to say and how you feel about it in precisely your own tone of voice, just as you do by inflection and rhythm when you speak. I think this is what T. E. Hulme meant when he wrote, "Freshness convinces you, you feel at once that the artist is in an actual physical state." Hulme was talking about Imagism—a fashion long past—but what he had to say about freshness, precision, zest, and openness to experience still applies and always has. When a writer is given over to a work in this way, the reader recognizes it and responds accordingly with a fresh take on the world and a renewed sense of being alive in his own skin. But the freshness is all in the execution, and it has nothing much to do with personality or performance. It depends, instead, on the kind of creative indifference or impersonality that Coleridge called "aloofness"—the ability to be at once deeply moved and detached, combined with the artisan's canny and practical understanding of what is needed to get the job done properly.

I wouldn't want to romanticize the figure of the artist. Art is a quest for order and sanity undertaken by people who are themselves often disorderly, none too sane, and rarely loveable. Mercifully, art itself is greater than the sum of the artists. To create voices in the reader's head, images in the mind's eye, imaginary presences with lives of their own is an intricate and subtle skill that requires self-awareness and self-denial—modesty, even—as well as a craftsman's fascination with the work as something with a life of its own, independent of its maker and his noisy ego. And this is not an image of the artist that comes easily in an age of personalities, showbiz, and promotion, when people are less interested in "it," the work, than in what's in it for them.

But then, the foreground of the literary scene is crowded with figures whose reputation dies with them, while the real writers get on with their work in the background. And that is how it has always been. Back in the seventeenth century, for example, the poems of John Cleveland, an absurd Cambridge don whose outlandish conceits destroyed the reputation of the Metaphysical poets for generations, went through twenty editions, thirteen of them in two years, while Milton's first collection of poems was reprinted once.

Bad art is always with us, taste is unpredictable, fame unreliable, and only history, as they say, will be our judge. In the meantime, it is the business of writers to create as true a voice as they can—if only to show themselves that it can be done, and in the hope that someone out there is listening.

ACKNOWLEDGMENTS

This book is based on three lectures given at the New York Public Library in October 2002. In expanding the last lecture, I have incorporated material from my introduction to *The Faber Book of Modern European Poetry* (1992); from "Drugs and Inspiration," first published in *Social Research* in 2001; and also from "The Myth of the Artist," originally delivered as the Hopwood Lecture at the University of Michigan and published in *Michigan Quarterly Review* in 1980, and, in a revised version, in *Madness and Creativity in Literature and Culture*, edited by Corinne Saunders and Jane Macnaughton (London: Palgrave Macmillan, 2004).

NOTES

Chapter 1. Finding a Voice

1 John Cheever, *The Journals*, Jonathan Cape, London, 1991, p. 128.

2 Sigmund Freud quoted by Lionel Trilling, "Authenticity and the Modern Consciousness," *Commentary*, New York, September 1971, Vol. 52, p. 39.

3 Samuel Taylor Coleridge, *Biographia Literaria*, Everyman's Library, J. H. Dent, London, 1952, p. 150.

4 Sigmund Freud, *Recommendations to Physicians Practising Psychoanalysis*, Standard Edition, Hogarth Press, London, 1964, Vol. 12, p. 111.

5 Coleridge, *Biographia Literaria*, p. 154.

6 Philip Roth, *Patrimony*, Simon & Schuster, New York, 1991, p. 237.

7 Sigmund Freud, *Studies on Hysteria*, Standard Edition, Hogarth Press, London, 1964, Vol. 2, pp. 160–61.

8 Sylvia Plath, *Collected Poems*, Faber & Faber, London, 1987, pp. 289–90.

9 T. E. Hulme, *Speculations*, Routledge & Kegan Paul, London, 1936, pp. 238, 231.

10 Hulme, "Romanticism and Classicism," *Speculations*, pp. 132–33, 135–36.

11 Isaac Babel, "Guy de Maupassant," *The Collected Stories*, World Publishing, New York, pp. 331–32.

[12] Alice Munro, "The Bear Came over the Mountain," *The New Yorker*, December 27, 1999.

[13] W. H. Auden, *The Dyer's Hand*, Faber & Faber, London, 1962, p. 287.

[14] Edith Wharton, *A Backward Glance*, Century Hutchinson, London, 1987, pp. 242–43.

[15] George Orwell, "Politics vs. Literature," *Collected Essays*, Secker & Warburg, London, 1968, Vol. 4, p. 221.

[16] Ford Madox Ford quoted by Ian Hamilton, *The Trouble with Money*, Bloomsbury, London, 1998, p. 142.

[17] Virginia Woolf, letter to V. Sackville-West, March 19, 1926, *Congenial Spirits, The Selected Letters of Virginia Woolf*, edited by Joanne Trautmann Banks, Harcourt Brace Jovanovich, New York, 1990, pp. 204–5.

Chapter 2. Listening

[1] Samuel Taylor Coleridge, *Biographia Literaria*, p. 153.

[2] I. A. Richards, *Principles of Literary Criticism*, Routledge, London, 2001, p. 127.

[3] T. E. Hulme, "Romanticism and Classicism," *Speculations*, pp. 135–36.

[4] A. Alvarez, *Night: An Exploration of Night Life, Night Language, Sleep, and Dreams*, W. W. Norton, New York, 1995, p. 179.

[5] Barbara Everett, "Donne and Secrecy," *Essays in Criticism*, Vol. 51, No. 1, January 2001, p. 52.

[6] Albert Einstein quoted by Roger Penrose, *The Emperor's New Mind*, Vintage, London, 1990, p. 548.

[7] Alfred Brendel, *The Veil of Order*, Faber & Faber, London, 2002, pp. 190, 45.

[8] Hulme, *Speculations*, p. 242.

[9] Richards, *Principles of Literary Criticism*, p. 127.

[10] Les Murray quoted by Peter F. Alexander, *Les Murray: A Life in Progress*, Oxford University Press, Melbourne, 2000, p. 135.

[11] Roland Barthes, *Writing Degree Zero*, Jonathan Cape, London, 1967, pp. 16–17.

[12] Frank Kermode, *Shakespeare's Language*, Allen Lane, Penguin Press, London, 2000, p. 187.

Chapter 3. The Cult of Personality and the Myth of the Artist

[1] George Moore quoted by John Crowe Ransom, "Poetry: A Note in Ontology," *The World's Body*, Scribner's, New York, 1938, p. 125.

[2] William Phillips and Philip Rahv, eds., *The New Partisan Reader*, Harcourt Brace, New York, 1953, p. vi.

[3] William Empson, *Seven Types of Ambiguity*, Chatto & Windus, London, 1949, p. 9.

[4] Italo Calvino, *If on a Winter's Night a Traveler*, Vintage, London, 1998, pp. 235–36.

[5] Zdzislaw Najder quoted by A. Alvarez, *Under Pressure*, Penguin, Harmondsworth, 1965, p. 21.

[6] George Orwell, "Politics and the English Language," *Collected Essays*, p. 137.

[7] Philip Roth, *Shop Talk*, Houghton Mifflin, Boston, 2001, p. 42.

[8] Miroslav Holub, "Poetry against Absurdity," *Poetry Review*, Summer 1990, p. 6.

[9] Edmund Wilson, "Historical Criticism," *Critiques and Essays in Criticism*, selected by Robert Wooster Stallman, Ronald Press, New York, 1949, p. 457.

[10] Phillips and Rahv, *New Partisan Reader*, pp. vi–vii.

[11] Mary McCarthy, *On the Contrary*, William Heinemann, London, 1962, p. 18.

[12] Philip Rahv, *Image and Idea*, New Directions, New York, 1957, p. 1.

[13] Allen Ginsberg, *Journals*, Penguin, London, 1996, p. 339.

[14] Norman Mailer, *Advertisements for Myself*, Signet, New York, 1960, p. 335.

[15] Althea Hayter, *Opium and the Romantic Imagination*, Faber, London, 1968, p. 19.

[16] Samuel Taylor Coleridge, *Poems,* Oxford University Press, Oxford, 1957, p. 296.

[17] Holub, "Poetry against Absurdity," pp. 4–5.

[18] Allen Ginsberg quoted by Ian Hamilton, *Against Oblivion*, Viking, London, 2002, p. 264.

[19] Elizabeth Hardwick, *Seduction and Betrayal*, Weidenfeld & Nicholson, London, 1974, p. 107.

[20] Randall Jarrell, "Bad Poets," *Poetry and the Age*, Faber, London, 1955, p. 160.

[21] Empson, *Seven Types of Ambiguity*, p. 205.

[22] Hanna Segal, "A Psychoanalytic Approach to Aesthetics," *The Work of Hanna Segal: A Kleinian Approach to Clinical Practice*, J. Aronson, New York, 1981.

[23] T. S. Eliot, "Tradition and the Individual Talent," *Selected Essays*, Faber, London, 1951, p. 21.

[24] John Berryman quoted by John Haffenden, *The Life of John Berryman*, Routledge & Kegan Paul, London, 1982, p. 382.

[25] John Berryman, *Recovery*, Faber, London, 1973, p. 96.